THE ENFORCER

The Story of "Happy Jack" Burbridge

by JACK BURBRIDGE
as told to Victoria Chandler

With Foreword by Pat Boone

published by
ACCLAIMED BOOKS
Box 18186
Dallas, Texas 75218

Acclaimed Books
Box 18186
Dallas, Texas 75218

Copyright © 1980 by Jack Burbridge
First Edition

ISBN 0-932294-09-X
Library of Congress Catalog Card Number: 80-6987-2

Printed in the United States of America

All rights reserved. No portion of this book may be reproduced in any form, except for brief quotations in reviews, without the written permission of the publisher.

Scriptures quoted in this book are from the KING JAMES VERSION.

Distributed by Acclaimed Books, Box 18186, Dallas, Texas 75218

DEDICATION

I gratefully dedicate this book
to my wife, Carolyn,
and my two children, Jackie and Vern,
who loved me through it all.

Foreword

"I've been in a number of prisons.

Attica, less than a year after the bloody riots.

San Quentin, a couple of times, the second time with my whole family. A number of other prisons, maximum and minimum security, with and without musicians.

When I go in, I always follow Johnny Cash's advice, "just tell them you care, and don't preach to them." Johnny knows what he's talking about, and confided that most of the prisoners, male and female, would figure I had some kind of "angle", and be suspicious of me. He said that just going in, singing and *caring* enough to be there would be sermon enough.

I usually go at least one step further and let them know that it's because I'm a Christian that I care.

In the back of my mind, I'm always remembering that Jesus *promised* He would ask us, when we stood before Him in that last day "when I was sick and in prison—where were you? Did you visit me?"

The part of that, that gets me is that Jesus identifies with the prisoner! And after many visits, I'm beginning to understand why.

There are Jesus people in every prison.

In many cases, they were Christians before they got there, but didn't allow Jesus to guide their lives. They allowed the flesh, the lure of material things, the appetites and dictates of human nature or the influence of friends to drag them down. But they *are* born again people who have fallen on the rocks.

Others have become believers while *in* prison. In almost every correctional facility or prison in the United States, Jesus has His people and is working there just as actively as anywhere else in our society. And in His ministry and in His teaching He seems more concerned about the prisoner, the naked and the hungry and the sick than any of the "well folks".

That's where Happy Jack comes in.

If you ever needed a dramatic example of how much Jesus loves the unlovable, and how He can transform the most "hopeless" case into a loving and useful servant— Happy Jack is it.

I met Jack Burbridge some years back, and was impressed with the dramatic change in his life and the glow in his face. It was hard for me to imagine that his former life had been as sordid and violent as he said it was, but it was that, and more.

Maybe Jesus uses people like Jack as wonderful examples that He can change *anybody*, that no one is beyond His redemptive power and His limitless grace. I think you'll get many a thrill, and shed a few tears, as you travel along the road with Jack.

He deserves the name "Happy Jack"—because he's got everything in the world to be happy about. And I think *you'll* be happier too, as you share in the good things Jesus has done for and through him."

1 Corinthians 4:20

Pat Boone, Beverly Hills
California

Contents

THE ENFORCER

CHAPTER ONE

Stealing Blood

Clink.

The sound of metal on metal broke the stillness of a dark street in Mishawaka, Indiana. A hub cap clattered on the pavement.

"Hey! Who's out there?" A man's voice came suddenly out of the darkness.

"Let's go!" my buddy whispered, his voice frantic. "Somebody heard us! Hurry!"

Our footsteps echoed on the sidewalk as lights flickered on in a nearby house. We vanished down the block, running as fast as we could.

"Do you think he saw us?" one of my friends asked when we finally stopped to catch our breath.

We waited for someone to follow. But no one did.

I was just 13 years old when I began stealing hub caps with my friends. By the time I was 15 years old, I was stealing the whole car. By the age of 21, I was an enforcer for organized crime; by the age of 29, I was a bank robber, heroin addict and next in line for the FBI's 10 Most Wanted List.

My life would be a strange one for a man whose mother had given him to God when he was still a tot in diapers.

One day my Mom had taken her two year old toddler in her arms and prayed, "Lord, I dedicate this child to Your service." God had answered, she said, promising that one day I would be His servant.

Over the years, Mom had to hold on to that promise, but she never doubted. God had *promised* and she believed Him. Each time she heard about a new eruption of violence in my life, or read another headline about yet another crime I had committed, she prayed, "When, Lord? *When. . .?*"

When I was eight years old, my Dad came home from the service and trouble came with him. It was 1945 and Dad had seen a lot of war. He had been gone for so many years that Mom had trouble turning the family over to him again—she had been head of the house too long. Their reunion started an argument that lasted for three years, until they finally called it quits.

While Dad was in the service, Mom had worked as a nurse's aide at the local hospital. With both parents gone, Johnny, my big brother, and I were alone together constantly. He became best friend, teacher and father to me. He was my idol and I was his shadow. Johnny taught me, guided me and loved me—and when we were separated, the first seeds of rebellion took root in the fertile soil of anger and hurt.

I stood on the steps of the school one sunny afternoon waiting for Johnny to pick me up. Johnny always came for me, but each afternoon, I could hardly wait to see him again. As his 1922 Franklin pulled up at the sidewalk, I ran to the car in excitement, but when I opened the door, I saw that he was crying. Silently, I slipped onto the seat beside him and watched the tears rolling down his cheeks. "Who would have hurt Johnny and made him cry?" I wondered angrily. When he finally spoke, his voice sounded distant and strange.

2

"Mom and Dad. . .couldn't make it," he said slowly. "I have to go with Dad. You're staying with Mom."

The words rang in my ears. What did it mean? Dad had divorced Mom, Johnny explained, but they hadn't separated us. That was the *judge's* decision.

The judge? A judge was somebody who sentenced murderers to the electric chair and made bad men go to prison. Why would a judge want to take Johnny away from me? I stared out the window at the familiar sights of kids walking home from school; at the sidewalks bustling with people who disappeared into the stores and then reappeared behind the decorated windows. I suddenly felt alone—and terrified.

Johnny took me home, as he always did. But this was the last time. I stood on the sidewalk crying as I watched his car vanish around the corner.

At first, I couldn't accept the fact that one man, a judge, could have the power to separate Johnny and me. But I gradually understood. When a judge spoke a few words, pounded his gavel a couple of times, everyone had to obey him. I didn't understand all the adult reasons for the divorce—all I knew was that the judge had torn my young life apart. *He* was against me. He wanted to destroy me. He hated me—so I hated him back with an anger I had never known before.

Mom and Dad still went to the same church they had attended together before and Johnny and I were caught in the middle. It was painful for me to watch Dad and Johnny sitting across the church from Mom and me each Sunday. I didn't understand why things had to be this way. Church, I decided, was an uncomfortable place, a place to be avoided. Sitting in church, to me, meant being hurt.

So I started sneaking out. Our church, Midway Tabernacle in Mishawaka, was the old-fashioned kind where praying could go on half the night. That gave some

3

of us kids plenty of time to find something *fun* to do. Some of our folks were in the choir facing us, but the congregation was so large that no one would notice a couple of skinny boys slipping down the aisle. And since it was a Pentecostal church, everyone had their hands raised and eyes closed; no one would be looking around anyway.

One by one, we slipped out and met in the parking lot behind the church. The first night, we stuck to the church grounds, but the second night, we got up enough nerve to go down to the amusement park two blocks away. And we really played the scene, strolling up and down the walkways, watching people shoot wooden rabbits or plastic fish for prizes. The lights, the music, the sound of laughter, and the bright colors—it was exciting to me. It was harmless enough, except for one thing—I didn't have enough money. The quarter that Mom had given me for the offering plate didn't go very far in the park.

The next week, all my friends, except me, backed out. They decided that sooner or later they'd get into trouble with their folks, but that didn't bother me. Anything would be better than having to sit in church. I had my first taste of freedom and I liked it. And anyway, it didn't take me long to decide that church people, especially Mom, were weirdos just doing their thing. If Mom wanted to waste half the night in church, *fine*; but I was going to the park.

One Sunday night, the inevitable happened. I didn't make it back to church in time and I found Mom waiting in the parking lot for me. When she found out about my escapades, she was hurt. What did she do? She *prayed*.

Mom was one of those "prayer warriors" who figured that the solution to every problem was prayer—hard prayer. When I was older and came home in the middle of the night, I braced myself as I opened the front door. I knew Mom would be praying. The minute I stepped in the house, I'd hear a loud, agonizing voice, "Lord! *When* are

4

you going to save my son? Lord! Change my boy . . ." I'd turn the TV and radio on full blast, slam pots and pans around the kitchen, stomp and make any racket I could to drown out the sound of those prayers.

I didn't need anyone praying for me and I didn't want God or anybody else to change me. For years, I flew into a rage whenever anyone said they were praying for me. One night, Mom confronted me in the kitchen about something I had done, and she ended by saying, "Son, I'm praying for you." It infuriated me, and I wheeled around and put my fist through a cabinet door, an inch from her jaw.

Mom believed in prayer and trying to tell her that prayers were in vain was like trying to tell a little boy that the sky isn't blue. Through the years, Mom remained undaunted. Her whole attitude toward me summed up in two words—*God promised.*

Soon after my church friends chickened out, the two of us who were still going to the park found some new friends—ones who wouldn't chicken out and didn't go to church anyway. One of the boys, Jim, a freckled-face red head with an Irish temper, had been friends with me since elementary school. Years later, we would still be friends— as partners in organized crime and one of the most dangerous teams in the mid-west. But for now, we were just a couple of kids trying to figure out where we could pick up a buck or two.

When we stole our first set of hub caps, it was just for a prank. The safest parking lot I could think of was the lot behind my church. We didn't even have to be quiet there. We lifted a set of hub caps, wore them like hats and danced around the parking lot. When we moved to the amusement park and clowned around some more, a man approached us to ask if the hub caps were for sale.

"Hey kids," the man whispered to us, motioning us over

5

into the shadows. "Are those hub caps you got for sale? I'll give you a dollar for the set."

We had been wondering how we could get some money, so we accepted the man's offer eagerly. The man told us he wouldn't mind having a few more hub caps sometime; he'd even like a few "extras" too, like radios, tires, fender skirts . . . and he'd pay a lot more than a dollar. For the next few months, we stole hub caps and "extras" but within two years we had graduated to wholesale car theft. We stole the cars, stripped them and sold the parts to the man in the park and some other men. They got what they wanted and we got what we wanted.

When I entered high school, I discovered a talent that would become my career—violence. I had always been a good fighter, because Johnny and his friends were six years older than me and I had to learn to fight if I wanted to go around with them. But I had always had a mean streak, too, even when I was a little kid.

When I was just six years old, I put our paper boy in the hospital. Every day when I was out in the yard playing after school, the paper boy would try to hit me with our paper as he rode by on his bike and he usually succeeded. One day when I saw him coming, I dragged a snow shovel behind a tree and when he rode by, I jumped out and swung the shovel with all my might. The bike went in one direction, the boy went in another, and papers flew all over the street. Everyone thought that I hadn't really meant to hurt him, but they were wrong. I wasn't sorry at all when the ambulance came.

But now I was in high school, and bigger. And meaner. I wasn't a bully, but I could take care of myself. One day a black guy stabbed me in the knee and I threw him down a flight of concrete stairs. When he landed at the bottom right in front of a door just as the teacher was stepping out into the hall, I got expelled. I didn't think it was fair, but

6

then I knew the authorities never were fair. I got expelled again when a teacher hit me on the hand with his stick for having a comic book hidden in my math work book. He meant to knock the book out of my hand, but he missed and came down on my knuckles. I reacted on instinct—I jumped up and slugged him.

My rebellion against authority was worse in sports. I was on the school swimming team and as a sophomore won second place in the state championship in diving, qualifying for the Junior Olympics. I didn't have too much trouble with my temper in the swimming competitions, but basketball was another story. I was on the school basketball team, but I never finished one game in all the years I played. I was either thrown out for poor sportsmanship, usually because I started a fight, or I fouled out for "playing dirty."

At the same time, I was an honor student. The teachers had to give me the grades I earned, even though my "citizenship" was hopeless. I was even offered rides to college, as we called scholarships—I didn't see anything ironic about being an honor student by day and a car thief by night. Mom and my teachers hoped I'd go on to college, but I had other plans.

It was the 1950's, the era of the leather jackets, duck tails and motorcycle gangs. I had it all. I had already made up my mind what I wanted to be. My hero was the James Cagney type gangster and I wanted to be just like him—a top gangster, not just a thug.

But I couldn't start my "career" as long as I stuck around home; so I decided to take off. One afternoon after school, three of us—a friend, my girlfriend, and I—jumped in a car and headed for Florida with big dreams of becoming rich and famous criminals. Naturally, we didn't get very far. We didn't even get out of the state before we ran out of money.

In Indianapolis, we found a little corner grocery that looked safe, and I went in and pulled a knife on the clerk—who turned out to be an off-duty *cop*. Within minutes I found myself in a cold dreary jail cell staring through a set of bars. And I was scared, really scared, for the first time in my life. I hated the chill, the glaring light from a single bulb, the smell of dried urine. Shivering and miserable, I sat slumped on a cot, watching the cops fill out the papers at the front desk. I wished I had never left home.

When the police found out that I was a good kid from a nice home, and even an honor student, they decided the grocery store incident was just a matter of "poor judgment" on my part. They figured I was just a scared kid who got carried away with the thrill of running away from home, and I assured them they were right. I *was* just a scared kid. I could walk out, they told me, but only on the condition that I went back to school. I was ready to agree to anything to get out of that place.

A couple of hours later, Mom and Dad both walked in the jail looking very solemn. I sheepishly followed them out to the car and we rode in silence all the way back home.

The experience had a sobering effect on me. Maybe being a criminal wouldn't be so great after all, I told myself, since I might end up in jail; I never wanted to step foot in a jail again. I did straighten up. I stopped stealing cars and I behaved myself perfectly—for about a month. When the scare was over, I settled back into my old ways, because I wanted more money again, as always.

Mom never had given me the kind of money I wanted, and anything over a few dollars, I had to get for myself. Most kids who steal are either the "have nots" who steal partly out of need; or the "haves" who steal because they enjoy it—that was me. I had everything I needed and many of the things I wanted, but I liked stealing. I already had what the adults called "stealing blood."

Stripping cars was a dirty, greasy job, and my friends and I wanted something cleaner and easier. If a cop had spotted us, we would have had a hard time explaining why we were covered with grease from head to foot in the middle of the night. After checking out the possibilities, we decided to burglarize appliance stores. It was quick, easy work that kept us in good money for over a year—until the cops arrested a couple of the guys in the ring the morning after a job.

I decided that now was the time to make my break with home. When the guys were arrested, I was afraid they'd tell the cops everything. I was sure they would, and I wasn't about to stick around to go to jail again. The only thing I could do that would give me both an income and a ticket out of the area was the service.

The guys were arrested early one morning; that afternoon, I was on a bus headed for boot camp. The recruiting offices for all the branches of service were lined up in a row and I began with the first one—the Navy. The Navy couldn't get me out of the area soon enough; the Marines didn't need anybody right then; but the Air Force had room for four more guys in a group leaving immediately. If I hurried, I could make it.

I was only 17 years old, but Mom was so rattled that she signed the papers stating I was 18. I was big for my age anyway, so the recruiting officer didn't have any trouble believing me.

The sun was going down when the bus crossed the Indiana border, heading for Texas. I was on my way.

CHAPTER TWO

Training

"Burbridge, you got the right temperament," a rough-looking sergeant barked. He looked me over, slapped me on the back and made me squad leader two weeks after I arrived at Lackland Air Force Base in San Antonio, Texas.

By "the right temperament," he meant that I was as mean as a snake. I started fighting almost the minute I arrived and didn't stop for three years. Big and hot-tempered, I'd take on anybody, any time, any place. It helped a lot when I went from 182 to 210 lbs. during basic training—I added 30 lbs. of muscle to a 6'3" frame—and nobody could beat me.

In the base championship boxing matches, I emerged as the winner and was scheduled to a match with the winner of another Texas base for the Division Championship Title. The day arrived, the bell rang, I went out to meet my opponent, and the last thing I remembered was a glove in my face. The glove belonged to a guy twice my size and just as fast. He won by decision, because he beat me to a pulp, but I wouldn't stay down. I knew I was getting mutilated, but I was determined to last all three rounds. When the last bell rang, after what seemed like an eternity of getting punched in the face, I was taken to the infirmary.

It was one of the few times I ever lost a fight. Instead of deciding I'd better back off from fighting, since it *could* be dangerous and I *might* get hurt seriously someday, I just decided I'd be meaner and faster than the other guy so I wouldn't get hurt. It wasn't long before I learned karate and another more exotic form of martial arts. With these new skills in violence, I just got tougher and more hot-headed. If I kicked a man in the teeth for looking at me wrong, what could he do about it?

Home on Christmas leave that year, I met a man I would encounter many times over the years. He was Ralph Wolfe, a cop who would take more than a casual interest in my life.

It was snowing that holiday night when I drove to a bar in South Bend to party and hear an all-girl band the bar was advertising. The warmth of the bar and the bourbon felt good after the bitter cold outside. After a few drinks, I decided to have fun with one of the band members by throwing pennies in her saxophone. I liked watching her as she tried to avoid the coins. Some of the guys were laughing and cheering me on; but some weren't. Not only was I distracting the girl while she was trying to perform, but the coins put tiny dents in her shiny sax.

"I wouldn't do that if I were you." I heard a threatening growl behind me. Pretending to ignore the warning, I brought my hand up as if to flip another penny, but instead I caught the guy under the chin with my elbow. I heard the sharp crack of his teeth as he went flying backwards.

I didn't know that the guy was a Notre Dame student— or that half the guys in the bar were too. I didn't mind, though. The city boys like me had a running feud (over the local girls) with the "rah rah boys," as we called Notre Dame guys.

A rah rah boy took a swing at me, but I was too fast.

11

Within 30 seconds, everyone in the bar was taking a shot at somebody and soon we were having an old-fashioned donnybrook. The girls in the band were screaming and the manager was running around yelling for us to stop. In the middle of the fun, I heard the faint sound of an approaching siren, and I gradually moved toward the back door. I thought it best that the cops not find me there.

When I flung open the back door, I almost fell over a cop. A baby-faced rookie was just coming in. He looked like he had been polished and his uniform couldn't have been more than a few hours old. I stared at him for a split second, but caught completely off guard at the sight of a cop, I drew back my fist and sent him flying through the snow.

Immediately, I heard the "click" of a gun being cocked, and I froze. The rookie's partner, an old veteran, was standing about a yard away, with his gun aimed directly at my heart. He started to motion me toward the patrol car, but to my amazement, the rookie picked himself up, brushed the snow off his new uniform and yelled, "This is mine!"

Ralph, in his policeman's uniform and I, in my Air Force uniform were having a regular street fight. No matter how hard I hit, Ralph came back. He'd stagger from a blow, then come at me in a flying tackle. When he couldn't get a blow in, he just grabbed handfuls of muddy snow to throw in my face. He was furious!

Soon, a crowd gathered around to cheer us on, some for me and some for Ralph. I'd hear, "Get that cop!" or "Come on! You can beat a prop head!" Guys piled up three and four deep around the circle and hooted, yelled and hollered.

About 20 minutes into the fight, another patrol car came screeching to a halt nearby with siren and lights going full blast. A police lieutenant and a sergeant jumped out and broke through the crowd.

"That's enough of this!" the lieutenant yelled angrily. He was disgusted, not with me, but with his rookie. He turned to me first and spit the words, "Get outta here!" Then he turned to Ralph and grumbled under his breath, "I'll see *you* in the morning." I picked up my hat and walked away, leaving Ralph so mad that he was red-faced and shaking like a leaf. His behavior had been so "unprofessional" that they couldn't arrest me, even though I had started the fight.

I found out later that Ralph had just graduated from rookie school and this was his first assignment as a police officer with the South Bend PD. I was never satisfied that I had beaten him, but he was. He felt disgraced and we both wanted to settle the fight. From that night on, we had a personal vendetta that would at times be humorous, but at other times serious—dead serious.

After basic training, I was shipped to Wiesbaden Air Force Base in Germany, where I had further training—but not for the Air Force. I hadn't been in Germany but a few days before I discovered that the little frauleins were only too willing to play all kinds of games with the American soldiers, and I began a lucrative business in prostitution. I had done some amateur pimping before, but now the profits were considerably higher.

I soon got involved in a host of black market activities and was making money hand over fist. And I was having a great time. I played drums in the base band (twice for Elvis when he was on tour in Germany as a soldier), wrecked cars for guys who wanted to collect the insurance money, raced, gambled, and, as always, fought. I got into one scrape after another, had a summary court martial for my "attitude," and was always in one kind of trouble or another.

13

I was a natural for violence, mainly because I was so fast. My reactions were like lightning. I could make a $100.00 a night by betting guys in a bar that I could drop a playing card and catch it before it hit the floor. They said it couldn't be done, so they'd put down $10.00. And I'd just rake it in.

As a medic, my schedule was rough—on duty 24 hours, then off 48. I was exhausted after working a straight 24 hours, but it would often be another 24 hours before I could get to bed. I had too much business to handle. One day, after a few weeks of almost no sleep, a nurse suggested that pills were just what I needed. They could give me energy when I needed energy and sleep when I needed sleep. Barbiturates would do the job. She offered to get me some bennies. I was ripe.

First it was two pills to wake me up, then four, and soon I was popping them by the handfuls. I gulped down pills to get me going in the morning and pills to keep me going during the day and more pills to bring me down at night so I could get some sleep. But with bennies, I didn't need much sleep.

One day, I almost went to sleep forever. One overcast morning in September, I took my motorcycle to a race track to make a few jumps off the ramp. I had done some racing before and tried to stay in practice in Germany. I had to build speed up to 90 kilometers (about 68 mph) to clear the sand trap at the end of the ramp, and as I began riding faster and faster around the track, I noticed a German walking his bike along the sides. I didn't pay much attention.

Almost ready to go onto the ramp, I looked down to check my speed one last time. When I looked up, my heart jumped to my throat. The German had walked his bike directly in front of the ramp entrance, now only yards ahead. I had no time to react; and in a split second, I

14

crashed into him. I felt my body being crushed and then I was out.

Hours later, I was discovered under the bleachers several hundred feet away, a distorted mass of flesh and bone. An ambulance arrived and attendants loaded me on the stretcher, but I was pronounced dead. The German had already been taken away—to the mortuary. He had been cut in two.

As I was wheeled into the emergency room with a sheet pulled over my face, the ambulance attendant announced that he was bringing in a D.O.A. The medic on duty that shift, a friend of mine, walked over to see who had been killed, and when he pulled back the sheet, he gasped, "Oh no! Not Jack!" His cry attracted the attention of a doctor, who, out of curiosity, came over to look at me. As he bent over my body, he found a faint trace of life and he went to work.

The drab green walls of the hospital room seemed to expand and contract, as though the room was breathing. Faces were staring down at me through a fog. I heard a woman's voice echo distantly, "Hey, he's conscious. . ."

"I've wrecked my sports car," I told myself, "I've been injured in the accident. . . Mom's probably here. . ." I thought I was in the wreck I had had when I was 16 years old back in Indiana.

"Burbridge, you were in a motorcycle accident a few days ago." I was staring into the kind face of a doctor. "You were injured in a motorcycle accident, soldier . . . and you've got amnesia." Soldier? His words didn't make any sense to me.

My body was covered with casts and I looked like a mummy. Strings and wires and gadgets ran from my body to the stands that surrounded the bed. The multiple fractures, I was told, weren't the real problem. I had

15

several internal injuries and a severe head injury. The doctor told me sorrowfully that he couldn't see any way I could live.

Mom was notified of the accident, but advised not to try making a trip to Germany. I would be dead by the time she could get here. They assured her, however, that the body would be shipped back to Indiana for burial.

But slowly, I recovered. The days were endless rounds of pain and sleep, of faces staring down at me, then vanishing. Nurses poked and stabbed and wrote notes to the doctors. The doctors poked and stabbed and wrote notes to the nurses. "I'm sorry, Burbridge," I was told over and over, "it's only a matter of time." Finally, the day arrived when one doctor examined me and said, "Well, Jack, I guess you're going to make it after all."

One by one the casts were removed. But the pain stayed. After the doctors quit telling me I would die any day, they started telling me that I *couldn't* endure the pain. They finally decided I had an extremely high pain threshhold. From September when the accident occurred to February of the following year, I lived in intense pain night and day.

Most of the pain gradually left, except the headaches. The head injury left scar tissue on my brain, causing blinding headaches. The doctors said the only solution was brain surgery, but when they warned me that I'd have only a 40% chance of surviving, I told them "no thanks; I'll keep the headaches."

Even as I hobbled out of the hospital to be transferred back to the States, the doctors were still shaking their heads. I should have said, "You see, guys, I have this Mom back home in Indiana and she *prays* a lot. . ." But I didn't. I thought I had made it because *I* was tough. I never believed I would die in the first place.

I became so accustomed to pain that I couldn't imagine

16

being free from it. In the years to come, when guys would threaten to "hurt" me, I would laugh in their faces. I already hurt! As I crept out of the hospital door on a cane, I knew I could endure any pain now, and inside I was laughing. The man who can endure anything, I told myself, is afraid of nothing.

I could endure anything—except the pain inside, the pain that had nothing to do with my body. But it really hadn't begun to bother me yet. It cropped up every once in a while, but I pushed it aside.

CHAPTER THREE

Getting Organized

Soon after I was able to walk again, I was shipped back to the States for more treatment at Valley Forge Hospital in Pennsylvania. The doctors told me once again that I needed brain surgery, but I told them once again I'd rather keep the headaches.

Over the next ten years, the headaches would be frequent and agonizing. But for now, I was back to normal—in every way.

I was discharged from the hospital and the Air Force on the same day, in February, 1958. My superiors knew from my records that I had done everything illegal a soldier could do, and had been in trouble almost every day of my three years in uniform, but they still gave me a General Discharge under honorable conditions. I think they must have been glad to see me go and didn't want to delay my departure.

I had no plans, but I decided to go back to Indiana and find something, perhaps around Chicago. That night, I pumped myself full of pills to make the drive from Philadelphia to South Bend without stopping. I felt good. I had lost some weight, but most of my strength was back. I settled down in the seat of the sports car I had bought a few weeks earlier and headed out of town. I'd be home by morning.

As it turned out, I wouldn't be home for another year. On a sudden whim, I decided to stop for a quick drink at a bar I knew. When I went in and sat down, a middle-aged man who introduced himself as "Tony," struck up a conversation with me about his son who was still in the service. Soon, he was buying my drinks and telling me how much I reminded him of his son. A couple of hours later, he invited me for a night on the town, but when I told him again I was headed out, he insisted. "All the drinks on me!" he urged. "Come on—you can leave in the morning." Why not? I thought to myself; if he's got the money, I guess I could make the time.

As soon as we sat down at the first bar, the bartender walked over to us and slipped Tony a white envelope. I didn't think anything of it, until it happened again . . . and again. I wondered about it, but didn't want to ask questions.

When we walked into the fifth bar, again the bartender came up to us, but this one started yelling and cursing Tony, then suddenly slugged him. I was tanked up from several drinks on top of a handful of pills, and before I knew it, I had landed on the bartender and worked him over. When I straightened up my tie and returned to Tony, I noticed he was looking at me in a new light. He was grinning from ear to ear.

"Jack, howja like to earn 5 bills a week?" he asked the minute I sat down.

"Doing what? . . . who'd I have to kill?" I joked.

"Just do what you did then, that's all," he answered.

Five hundred dollars a week, I thought to myself, just for beating up bartenders? Tony had talked me into it.

My friend Tony turned out to be a chieftain in the Pennsylvania syndicate; that night, he hired me as an enforcer for his organized crime operations. I was ready for the job and I wanted the money.

My career was on the up. I was getting paid for doing what I always did for free. I rarely went to a bar without hurting somebody before the night was over anyway. This was a little different. I was supposed to walk up to a man who had never done anything to me and do a number on him, but I quickly discovered that all a guy had to do was say "no," and I'd get as mad as if he had kicked me in the teeth.

The syndicate had backed certain club or bar owners in the area with a "loan" and in return the operators had to turn over a percentage of their profits to the syndicate—to show their gratitude. Sometimes, an operator was tempted to hold back a little for himself, especially if he didn't have much to be grateful *with*. It was my job to persuade him to pay up and never try holding back again. I could be as brutal as I liked, just as long as I got the job done.

The day after Tony hired me, I was assigned a couple of prostitutes to manage. About a week later, I was given my first assignment for an act of enforcement. I did the job well and Tony was pleased. He had struck gold; so had I.

A few weeks into my career, I was sent to a club in Wildwood, New Jersey to do some enforcement and I ended up doing too much. The club was a front for prostitution and other operations, and the manager wasn't cooperating. When nothing I said convinced him to pay up, I got mad, started punching and just went crazy. I busted his shoulder with the butt end of the double barrelled shotgun I used and then shot up the place. The club looked like a tornado had hit it, and when I walked out, the manager was lying on the floor groaning.

The incident was a turning point in my career, because it gave me a reputation, which is almost as valuable as a gun in enforcement. The brutality of the incident alarmed the local police and suddenly I was the "dangerous new man" to East Coast crime operations. Across the nation, law enforcement agencies that kept tabs on organized crime activities sat up and took notice.

A few weeks later, I was in one of the syndicate clubs, as a client this time, when I overheard a man at the next table talking about some enforcer. "And you should have seen the club when 'Happy Jack' got through with it!" the man was saying. When he mentioned that the club was located in Wildwood, I realized that he was talking about me.

I had been nicknamed "Happy Jack," by some syndicate friends, because I snickered during an act of enforcement. I liked the name and it stuck! I *was* happy.

I knew enforcers didn't last long. For every enforcer that made it big in the syndicate, there were hundreds that were wasted before they were 30 years old. I was just a 21 year old kid with a lifetime in front of me. I *liked* the way my life was going. And besides, I didn't *think*—I reacted. I did whatever seemed to be the thing to do at the moment and whatever I did was right in my mind. It would be ten long years before I would realize that *perhaps* I wasn't a very nice person.

I may have been happy, but I made the enforcers in the neighboring areas very unhappy. Each group had to defend its own territory against other groups that wanted to expand. Power struggles were the name of the game, and I was stepping on toes right and left. Within a year, I had hurt too many people in my zealousness, and now it was time to take revenge. But I was too arrogant to be afraid.

With the amount of money and influence I had accumulated by then, I was assigned "errand boys" to work for me. We called them "gophers" ("go fer this, go fer that"); they were men who were working their way up the ranks of the syndicate, but were not yet skilled (violent) enough to go out on their own.

I had a big white Lincoln Continental that I never let anyone else drive. Not only was I proud of it—for the first time in my life I had big money, about $5,000 a month—but also it was too risky. The risks were always there, but I tried to be careful.

I had been staying in a hotel for the past few weeks and had my car parked in an alley beside the building. On that particular afternoon, I played cards until late, and now I had to start getting ready for a dinner date. On an impulse, I handed my keys to a gopher and told him to get the car gassed up and washed—I didn't have time.

I walked out the door with him, and he disappeared into the alley beside the building. As I turned to go back to my room, I heard a tremendous explosion and I knew immediately what had happened. My enemies had scouted the hotel and seen that my car had to be backed out, and they wired a bomb to the back-up lights. The second the man put the car in reverse, the bomb went off, and he lost his hearing, his sight and part of his shoulder

Because of my height, the bomb would have taken my head off. My enemies were sure I was a dead man that time, because they *knew* no one would be in that car but me. For days, a friend of mine just shook his head every time he saw me and said, "Hap, you're just damn *lucky!*"

Yeah, I was lucky alright, I thought to myself. I didn't know that my mother's God had His hand on me.

A few weeks later, the syndicate decided I needed to cool off, since both the cops and some of my colleagues were after me. I was transferred to my home area, to work part of the Chicago district. At last, I was going home.

CHAPTER FOUR

Not The Marrying Kind

I had seen Carolyn only once.

Dave, a friend of mine, and I were riding our motorcycles together one afternoon, when he asked me to drop by a restaurant with him; his wife worked there and he needed to see her for a minute. I went along and waited outside while he went in.

I took one look at a tall, lanky waitress through the restaurant's window and said to myself, "What a fox! I'm going after her . . ." It wasn't until Dave walked up to her that I realized *she* was his wife.

I wanted Carolyn as a prostitute—I was trying to expand my business and with her big brown eyes and blonde hair, Carolyn had what I was looking for. It didn't matter to me that she was married to Dave. Dave was okay, but Carolyn was fantastic.

I had a system I used to turn girls on to prostitution, and it usually worked. First, I talked a girl into going out, if not with me, then with her boyfriend or husband. If a guy was with her, I tried to get him drunk so I could make a play for the girl. If she turned out to be the right type, I began asking her questions, as tactfully as possible. I'd finally bring up the subject of money, mentioning how nice it would be to get paid for turning tricks instead of doing it for free. Most girls would finally say, "Well, yes, I guess I might as well . . ." After training, she'd be making good money within a month—for herself and me.

Later that week, when Dave and I were out drinking one afternoon, I tried to talk him into bringing Carolyn to the dance our motorcycle club was giving that night at the American Legion Hall. "We'll just have a few drinks," I told him, "and you and Carolyn can dance a little, then go home. Come on—it'll be fun." He said he'd think about it.

That evening, Dave was killed in a motorcycle accident. A car pulled out in front of him when he was doing about 60 mph.

Two days later, Dad, his new wife, and I went to the funeral home, where I was hoping to get a chance to talk to Carolyn. When we walked in, she was standing across the room near the casket, with a handkerchief in her hand, and I thought she was the most beautiful girl I had ever seen. We walked up to introduce ourselves.

"I'm Jack Burbridge," I said politely.

"Oh?" Carolyn answered. "You must be a friend of Dave's."

I had just made news in the South Bend Tribune and on all the television and radio stations for three weeks running. She should have reacted to my name. Most people did.

"You know, 'Happy Jack,'" I insisted, since the media had used that name.

"No . . ." she said, shaking her head, "Nice to meet you though."

This girl, I thought to myself as we left, is really dumb. She *had* to know my name. Anybody who partied, associated with a friend of mine, or did *anything* in the area knew who I was. Maybe, I said to myself, she was just trying to spare my folks the embarrassment of having a

24

stranger recognize my name. That must have been it. Any girl who could play it *that* cool really would make a good prostitute, I decided.

The situation had not eased up any since I had moved to the Chicago area, mainly because I hadn't let it. Within a month after arriving, I was in full operation, using a cigar store as a front. Ralph, the rookie cop I had fought in the snow four years earlier, had been notified that I was back, and he was out to get me for personal reasons, along with the rest of the cops who were out to get me for legal reasons. I needed to leave the area temporarily, so when my folks decided to go on a vacation to Arkansas, I decided to go with them. I would try to contact Carolyn when I got back.

Weeks later, I recognized Carolyn in her car when we passed on the highway. I waved, but she didn't wave back. For months, I waved or honked or smiled every time I saw her, but she never responded. When she didn't come to any of the syndicate clubs where everyone partied, I concluded that she wasn't the partying type and I let my interest in her slide.

I had almost forgotten about her when I walked into a nightclub one night in May and there she was, sitting at a table with a girlfriend—drinking. When she saw me, she looked very uncomfortable, and I thought it was because I had caught her in the act. I still thought she was a knock-out, and I headed straight for her table.

After we had talked for a few minutes, I asked her to dance, but to my amazement, she answered, "I don't know how to dance . . .I'm sorry." I didn't believe her, so I insisted, "Come on, I'll show you; there's nothing to it." I thought she was just being coy—until we got to the dance floor. She stepped all over my feet, but we both had a sense of humor and we kept trying until the music stopped.

25

"I suppose that you're going to tell me you're drinking 7-Up," I joked as we walked back to her table.

"But I *am* drinking 7-Up!" she protested. Again, I didn't believe her—until I took a drink from her glass. She was drinking 7-Up!

I didn't know any girls who couldn't dance and wouldn't drink. I couldn't believe she was for real. But I enjoyed her company in a way, so when the bar closed, we moved to an all-night restaurant where we laughed and talked for three hours. I was gradually convinced that she knew nothing about me or my way of life. But I still thought that maybe she was naive, but not innocent, and I wanted to put her to one last test—the sand dunes 40 miles away at Warren, Michigan.

As we rode to Warren, Carolyn didn't seem to mind that we were going there, but at the same time, she acted like she really hadn't caught on to *why* we were going there. Every girl knew what went on at the dunes, and the fact that Carolyn didn't say anything gave me hope.

But not for long. Carolyn was Miss Purity, and I finally gave up. It was no use—there was nothing to do with a girl like that but take her home.

"Tonight," she said as we drove back to South Bend, "is the first time I have laughed since Dave died—I really had a good time." I was glad. We talked and joked all the way home. When we were almost to her house and she invited me in for breakfast, one last suspicious thought crossed my mind, but when I turned into her driveway, I realized that she had moved home—with her folks.

Her Mom was an easy-going lady who didn't mind at all cooking eggs at 6:00 a.m. I soon found out why. She was used to it. I realized, when children started pouring into the kitchen from every corner of the house. I almost choked on my bacon when I counted them all—Carolyn was the oldest of 12 children!

As I drove home that morning, I decided I'd ask Carolyn out again, just for fun; she was so different that she was . . .interesting.

Family life had no attraction for me and I had vowed time after time that I would never get married. The nurse who had turned me on to pills had wanted to get married, but I lied and told her I'd been married before and I didn't like it. I like girls—a lot, but there was something about marriage that made a sweet, gentle girl start bickering and nagging at me all the time. I got enough hassles from my girls at work without marrying and getting hassled in my own home.

And then there was the matter of "my girls at work." Carolyn thought I ran a bar—that was okay with her; but telling a nice, moral girl like her that I was in prostitution would be like telling a Jew I was Hitler in disguise.

My mind wandered to the cigar store and the operations. I was on my way to the top and making more money than ever. Most of the girls in the area wanted to work for me, because I treated them like ladies. Some girls, however, didn't want to be treated like ladies—they thought my girls were candies because I didn't beat them up all the time. I insisted on having only nice girls, not sluts, and my girls *had* to act like ladies. The only time I ever hit a girl was when she started acting like a man.

I yawned and blinked at the 9:00 o'clock sun reflecting off a windshield. No, I told myself, my girls were a business, an important and honorable business and they were professionals. If I ever lost my mind and got married, it would be to one of my girls, who shared my way of life; I'd never marry a girl like Carolyn. A woman like her could put up with a lot—but not prostitution. Carolyn was sweet, but spacy. I'd ask her out that night, but I'd set her straight—she was the kind of girl who had marriage on her mind.

27

That night I bluntly told Carolyn, "If you're looking for a husband, you've got the wrong man. Marriage doesn't fit my style. And even if you just want me to tell you I love you, you can forget that too. The only kind of love that is real is physical love. Like I said, marriage doesn't fit my style.

One month and six days later, Carolyn and I were married. On our third date, I told her I loved her. On our fourth date, I asked her to marry me.

I never did understand how it happened. It was as though I went to sleep in May single and woke up in June married. I think I made my mistake when I took Carolyn home to meet Mom. Mom took one look at her and loved her. I think Mom started praying.

On the day of the wedding, I decided to treat the whole thing as a lark. If I didn't like her after a few months, I'd just tell her to get out. We had a motorcycle wedding, complete with press coverage, but the wedding cake tasted like sawdust.

Carolyn had wanted to marry me, I knew, but she had never said a word. When I gave her my big lecture on our second date, she had just nodded her head and agreed with me. She had fallen in love with me already, she told me later, because I was easy-going and didn't seem to be trying to *seduce* her all the time. She liked the fact that everyone seemed to like me—I was "different" from other men. I didn't tell her just how different I thought she was!

I didn't tell her a lot of things. It would be a matter of years before she would find out the extent of my activities. She began to piece things together during the next couple of years, but she discovered only the tip of the iceberg. My decision not to tell her anything wasn't because I was ashamed or afraid that she would leave me—I just felt that her ignorance would protect her if the police or other enemies tried to pressure her for information. She was the only thing in my life outside of crime and I liked it that way.

My girls didn't believe I had really gotten married. They had heard me say too often, "marriage doesn't fit my style." After seeing me with Carolyn for the first time, one of my girls pulled me off to the side and asked if Carolyn was going to work with them. The first night I took Carolyn to a club after we were married, another of my girls ran up to me at the door, threw herself around me like she was mounting a horse and planted a kiss on my mouth. Carolyn just thought the girl was an old girlfriend, and I didn't tell her differently. No one else would tell her differently, either, because they knew what would happen to them if they did.

It was still a miracle that Carolyn didn't get suspicious. She may have been a little dumb, but she wasn't stupid. When she told one of her brothers that she was marrying me, he exclaimed, "*the* Jack Burbridge?" People made comments like, "Maybe marriage is just what he needs!" Dave's mother even wrote, "I can't understand why you would want to marry a man like that."

I put Carolyn in a little house in the middle of a cornfield outside South Bend, so she couldn't accidently hear about me. I made sure she had no contact with anyone in my circles, and I tried leading a double life. I tried to be a kind and loving husband—but I finally stopped pretending. Carolyn was happy, though, during those first years of marriage, and it was a good thing—Jackie, a little girl, came on March 24, 1961, nine months after we were married; Vern, named for my dad, came two years later, on March 18, 1963.

It wouldn't be long before Carolyn would realize that something was wrong with my "job". When she started calling the cigar store and asking for "Jack Burbridge," the party who answered usually said, "Who? Oh, you

29

mean J.D." She thought it was strange that people in my own store didn't call me by my real name, but she didn't ask about it. I used "J.D." or "Jack Drake," or any last name that started with a "d". Very few people not directly involved in my activities knew my real name.

Then she started getting strange telephone calls from men who left messages like, "Tell Hap it's all set," or "Tell J.D. we need a couple of girls for the weekend." When she asked what the messages meant, I told her it was none of her business."

One night, a couple of years after we were married, I took Carolyn out to a restaurant. When we walked in the door, the manager came running up to meet us, obviously upset.

"Now, Hap, you're not going to get mad tonight, are you?" he asked frantically. "I'll buy your drinks, *anything,* but please, don't get mad!"

I mumbled something to the effect that I'd try not to get mad, and hurried past him. Carolyn couldn't figure it out.

"If I were the manager of a restaurant," she commented when we sat down, "and somebody made trouble, I would just kick him out. He *is* the manager, isn't he? Why was he treating you that way?" I made a joke about my temper and dropped the subject.

Some time later, Carolyn did see me work a guy over in a restaurant one night. I didn't want to fight because she was with me, but a man challenged me and kept pushing. When I tried to ignore him, he figured I was afraid and he pushed harder. I finally gave up and worked him over. When I returned to our table, Carolyn's eyes were as big as saucers. By then, guys were always trying to make a reputation for themselves by beating me in a fight and I found myself having to defend my reputation constantly.

It wasn't long before I grew to really love Carolyn in my own way. I didn't grow up in a loving home, and I didn't know how to love my family. But I did know how to take Carolyn in my arms and make her feel special. She *was* special to me, but at the same time, I thought of her as a possession. I *owned* a car, guns, a home and a wife. As for my children, I was afraid of them. When they were babies, I wouldn't hold them because I was afraid I'd hurt them; when they were older, I couldn't talk to them as a daddy because we were strangers to each other.

I have always thought I married Carolyn because she was so unbelievably innocent. I thought she needed protection from life, and I thought I was the one to give it to her; but of all men, I was the worst possible choice. Many nights over the next years, she would lie in bed beside me at night weeping softly. I was either drunk, asleep or high; even when I did hear her, I thought she was crying just because women sometimes cry for no reason. I didn't know she was praying for me.

CHAPTER FIVE

The Two New Men . . .

When I answered the phone one afternoon, I heard the voice of my old childhood friend, Jim, who used to strip cars with me when we were kids.

We had kept in touch over the years. J.K., as he was called now, had served time for aggravated assault. When he got out, he'd gone to the waterfront in California—also as an enforcer, but in another line of work. He was big and hot-tempered like me, and he, too, had been transferred to the mid-west to cool off. We had both been back in the area less than a month.

When he called, J.K. told me about a job we had to do in Gary, about 65 miles away. Some Greeks weren't co-operating; they'd heard about the two new men, J.K. and J.D., and figured we'd be easier to get along with since we were young and relatively inexperienced.

That night, J.K. and I drove to Gary and did our first act of enforcement together. We never had any more trouble with the Greeks.

We decided we liked the way we worked together. We were a lot alike in many ways—both tall, fast, and mean. We had the same temperment. J.K. was the kind who would shoot first and ask questions later. I knew that if some guy walked up behind me, J.K. would shoot him in the back; he knew I'd do the same for him.

After we picked up our pay for the job on the Greeks, J.K. and I went through an Indian-style ritual that made us official blood brothers. It was a syndicate practice, but not many men did it —they had to mean business. In front of a witness, we ran the ring finger of the left hand—the wedding ring finger—across a sharp knife and held the cuts together to let the blood mingle. We then took solemn vows to avenge the death of the one who died first.

In the early 1960's, J.K. and I went through a power struggle between the Indiana and Ohio syndicates. Ohio was trying to move into Gary and South Bend, and some of their boys were selling "baseball tickets," a baseball gambling game, as an effort to break into the area. One afternoon, J.K. and I drove to Ohio to strike a blow at our enemies; the damage we did was extremely serious, and we knew the Ohio boys would be after us.

I was in the cigar store when I got the call—they had come for us. They had already shot and wounded two enforcers that J.K. and I had taken with us to Ohio that day, but the Ohio men had made a serious mistake—they thought the two enforcers were J.K. and me, and they thought they had killed them. The Ohio enforcers were in a bar in Gary now, and some of our girls would keep them busy until we could get there. Since they thought we were dead, they had let their guard down.

I contacted J.K. and we agreed to meet at the bar in separate cars, then regroup at the rest area outside the city. We had to move fast. I needed somebody to go with me to Gary and to keep the car running while I went into the bar. J.K. was taking his ace, but I didn't have anyone with me at the moment.

I looked around the bar, but there was nobody suitable —except one man, Jack Arnold, a freckled-face carrot top, who was, unfortunately, a law-abiding citizen. Jack knew that I was involved in some kind of shady business, but had no idea what it was. He just dropped by the store every once in a while to visit. I hated to ask him to go to Gary with me, but I had to have him.

"Jack, would you mind taking a trip to Gary with me?" I asked casually, "I have to take care of some business . . . it won't take long."

"Well, I guess so," he answered. "Are you sure we'll be right back?"

"Yeah, it'll just be a quick trip," I assured him.

J.K. and I pulled up in front of the bar about 30 minutes later, and burst in the door of the bar together. We did a number on the Ohio enforcers, busted the bar operator's shoulders and shot up his place. When everyone was down, we backed out the door, with our guns still drawn, and dove into the cars.

When I drove to the rest area doing 110 mph, Jack Arnold's face turned white, and his freckles stood out like red polka dots. As I turned into the rest area too fast, a tire blew, and we started skidding sideways toward the row of gas pumps. The station attendants scattered in all directions, but the man who was getting his car serviced just froze and stared at the big white Lincoln coming at his car. About ten feet away, I gave the car enough gas to pull out of the slide. When Jack followed me into the restaurant, he was shaking all over

Inside, J.K. and I went to the restroom to wash the blood off our hands. When we joined Jack at the table, he finally spoke.

"Well," he gulped, "that was a quick trip alright, but I don't want to make any more!"

J.K. and I laughed. It was a routine day for me. Throughout the power struggle, my life was one act of violence after another.

The reason I survived the power struggle was because I didn't take any chances. I always anticipated my enemies —I knew what I'd do if I were them—and I didn't let my guard down night or day. *Control,* being on the top of the situation, was the only way I stayed alive. All it took was one careless move and I'd be dead. I wouldn't eat in a restaurant unless I could get a table with my back to the wall, preferably in a corner where I had a full view of the room and the door. I never went to movies.

My violence was calculated too. I knew that a victim, after an act of enforcement, would pick up a shotgun and shoot me in the back when I walked away—if he could. I made sure he couldn't use his arms. If I didn't want a man to walk across the room to a telephone when I left, I made sure he couldn't walk—for a long time.

My biggest asset was still my speed. I could knock a man out and he would never see my fist coming. Most of the time, I could put a man in the hospital and walk away without a single blow on me. One night, the speed of my reactions saved my life.

Toward the end of the power struggle, J.K. and I went to a honky-tonk near Griffin one night to do an act of enforcement. As we backed out into the darkness, we heard a snarl behind us, "Hey punks!"

Four men were hiding around the corner of the building, waiting for us. They were just some guys wanting to make a name for themselves by killing us; they weren't even enemies. We knew that after a man yelled, "Hey punks," he wasn't going to throw snowballs.

As they stepped out into the open, all four opened fire. J.K. and I spun around and hit the ground, but I caught a bullet from a 357 magnum in my left arm. We started firing in the direction of the gunfire, and in the exchange, the man who got the first shot off at me was gunned down.

35

We saw three figures run into the darkness. The shoot out had lasted only seconds; then it was over.

The man who shot me had me dead center. If I had hesitated even a split second, I would have been shot in the back. I felt the blow, but I thought I was just winged. When I got in the car, however, I saw little spurts of blood shooting out of a clean hole in my jacket sleeve. J.K. took one look and started driving like a maniac. He knew the bullet had hit a major artery, and I could bleed to death within minutes. But I didn't think about the possibility of dying; I told J.K. that his driving would kill me if the bullet didn't.

J.K. got me to a doctor who handled injuries for the syndicate and kept them off the police record. The bullet, he told me, had gone through the flesh in my arm. If it had hit the bone, I would have lost my arm.

I was sure the cops would be after me as soon as the incident was reported, so I hid out at J.K.'s that night. When nothing happened by morning, I drove home, parked in front of the house and told Carolyn to pull the car around to the back—I couldn't because I'd been shot. She almost fainted, but I assured her that it wasn't serious.

A few days later, the police called me in for questioning. They had information that I had been shot in the right arm, not the left, so one cop came down on my right arm, expecting me to sail through the ceiling. "How's it going, Burbridge?" he asked casually. "Just fine," I answered, "Want to try the other arm?" Since I didn't react when he hit my arm, he figured I hadn't been shot after all.

The only people who could have identified me and place me at the bar at the time of the shooting *wouldn't*. They knew what I would do to them. I did so much damage to people who crossed me they knew I'd kill them—so I didn't have to.

36

Working in a high crime area like Chicago, I sometimes got mugged like everyone else. But when a guy attacked me, he got more than he bargained for and the results were funny.

One night, while I was stopped at a red light, a black guy jumped in the seat beside me and pulled a knife. He saw my Lincoln and figured I was some old rich man who'd be an easy mark.

"Man, I'm robbing you," he snarled.

"Oh yeah?" I pulled my gun and shot him in the knee. A look of shock crossed his face and he almost fell over himself trying to get out of the car. I heard him running down the street yelling, "He shot me! He shot me!" I think he was more surprised than hurt. He ran two blocks before he finally fell down.

Another time a beautiful black prostitute hopped into the car when I stopped for a red light. She started coming on to me and I laughed and reached over to the switch that locked all four windows electronically. She looked a little worried and said, "What you doing, man?"

"Well, if you're so eager to hustle," I explained, "I'm going to take you to my place and put you to work hustling for me."

"Who'er you?" she asked as her eyes got big.

"Happy Jack."

"*The* Happy Jack?"

She went to work for me and made a good prostitute. About a year later, I had to sell her because she started using drugs, something I never allowed.

One night three high school kids jumped me on a dark street. I took care of them, then took them to the police station and turned them in.

"I brought you three muggers," I said as I shoved the three kids into the station. "They jumped me." The cops had to laugh at the situation. They had no choice but to book the kids. Word got around the high school that the kids had tried to mug Happy Jack; the father of one of the boys actually came to apologize for his son.

Of course, I usually wasn't the "victim." When I was in a bad mood, which was almost all the time, I would punch some poor guy for no reason, and wind up in court the next day. One day a man honked his horn at me, and I got out of my car, pulled his head out of the window, punched him in the mouth, sending his false teeth flying. I drove off leaving the man hanging out the window with his false teeth on top of the car. Incidents such as that usually happened when I was mad at Carolyn. I didn't think it was manly to hit a girl, so when Carolyn made me mad, I would storm out of the house and hit anyone who came across my path. One night I had five different fights because I was mad at Carolyn. Violence was my way of relieving frustration.

After I would punch some guy who had done nothing to me but honk his horn or get in my way, I'd get a phone call the next morning. "Jack," my lawyer would sigh, "We have another assault and battery charge against you." I'd go into court and pay the fine, and walk out. We both got tired of the routine and it was costing me a lot of money, so I put an end to it. When he told me that someone had filed an assault and battery charge against me, I would find out who was filing it, go to his house and tell him to go down to court and drop the charges or he'd be hurt a lot worse next time. The charges were always dropped.

If a person didn't cross me, I was the best friend he could have. A guy who came out of prison knew he could come to Happy Jack for a T-bone steak. There was nobody I liked better than an underdog; it was *us* against the cops, the judges and the law. I had a strong sense of fair play that was unusual in my circles—or any circles for that matter. Some of my best customers for my prostitutes were judges and attorneys; the next day that same man might be sending a prostitute or pimp to prison.

I'd do anything for a friend who needed help—it was my way of thanking them. Sometimes, one of my girls would want out, and I'd let her go, with my blessing. Other guys would beat her up and tell her she'd be a prostitute until the day she died—which might be soon if she didn't straighten up. One of my girls came to me one day and said, "Jack, I really want out. My kids are getting older and I don't want them to know. . ." I told her that was fine, and that if she ever needed anything, to come to me. I couldn't do enough for friends—if they played it straight with me.

The other side of the coin was cruelty. One night a man used physical brutality on one of our girls. I heard a scream, went flying upstairs, and hauled the man outside. After I worked him over, I maimed him for life with a knife. I wanted him to remember me. Everytime he looked at his hands, I wanted him to remember that he tried to cross Happy Jack.

A nice old Salvation Army man came by the cigar store every week to collect donations from my customers. One week when he came in, I was annoyed and threw a $10.00 bill in his hat just to hurry him up. I didn't want my customers bothered with religion. When the old man saw the bill, he exclaimed gratefully, "Why, son, God bless you! I'll be praying for you . . ."

"Son, I'm praying for you . . . God promised and I'm praying for you . . ." Mom's words always brought back a flood of emotions. I felt the anger rise up inside, and I hit the old man, picked him up and threw him out the door.

A short time after I was shot, our cigar store was torched by some of my enemies. And the cops couldn't wait to rummage through the ashes. They were "frustrated"—they couldn't get anything on me. But they did *that* time, when they found all the evidence they wanted—

gun smuggling, prostitution, drugs—and discovered that one of my girls was in the United States illegally *and* a minor.

I was facing seven federal and state counts from the evidence found in the building. The bonds cost me $36,000, which the syndicate was glad to pay until I could pay them back. The money didn't bother me; the police *did*. It was bad enough that my enemies had scored a blow, without the cops harrassing me. It was robbery to take my $36,000.

If they thought they could do that to me and get away with it, they had another think coming. I'd get even; and I'd sure as hell get my money back. One way or the other.

CHAPTER SIX

The Thanksgiving Day Message

"Jack, let's move," Carolyn suddenly said one night. "Let's move to another city and start over . . . please."

You talk like a crazy woman!" I snapped.

Why should I want a new life? The old one was just fine with me. It was 1964, and I was only 27 years old. I was already ranked the #1 enforcer in the area, and the #3 enforcer in the entire mid-west—and I still had at least a couple of decades to go.

But Carolyn had started acting strange. A week later, she said, "Jack, your little girl is starting to school soon. What are you going to do when she finds out her daddy is a notorious criminal?"

"She'll be *proud of me*, when she finds out her daddy is #1 in his . . ." But Carolyn wasn't listening any more. She had turned away.

The pressure was mounting, from the police and from some syndicate enemies. After the seven charges from the cigar store fire, I had to "walk softly" for awhile. It didn't seem like a bad idea to move. For two years, I had been traveling to Albuquerque to set up syndicate operations there; we were new to the city and now we were having some trouble. I could move there.

"Okay, Carolyn, we're moving like you wanted to," I told Carolyn one night. "We're going to Albuquerque and start that new life you talked about." She hugged me and started packing.

I moved to Albuquerque and took over syndicate operations. I had been there only a couple of weeks, when the FBI "asked" me to pay them a visit at their downtown headquarters. I strolled into a room full of agents who looked extremely solemn.

"Hello, Mr. Burbridge," the chief agent said, as he stood to shake hands. But then he dropped the small talk and cleared his throat.

"If you think," he began in a calm, deliberate voice, "that you are going to operate here like you did in Indiana, you have another think coming. We have our guns ready and we will use them."

"Well, you had *better* have your guns ready and oiled," I answered coldly, "because that is exactly why I'm here. And your men had better be careful not to step off a curb in front of my car—my foot would accidently slip off the brakes and onto the gas. . ."

He jumped up. "Are you threatening federal officers?" he yelled angrily.

"No, *Sir*," I replied sarcastically. "I'm just giving you fair *warning*." I stood up and left.

I had plans. I bought a car dealership as a front for my operations and was moving full-steam ahead within a month.

On Thanksgiving Day, 1965, Carolyn sat on the step of our sunken living room, with her face in her hands. It was late afternoon, and she had been crying since morning. The children were out playing, running in every once in a while to ask why they weren't "having Thanksgiving" like other children. But there was no dinner, no friends, no

42

holiday cheer in our house. I had been asleep all day.

Other families, Carolyn thought to herself, were gathered around the table now, saying grace to God, enjoying each other. Not her family. *Her* husband was sleeping it off in the bedroom, she thought bitterly. She saw why we had moved to Albuquerque. Everything was the same as always; only the surroundings were different.

Carolyn had had enough. She was almost to the breaking point. She had been praying for me all the years we had been married. She was a member of the Reorganized Church of Jesus Christ of the Latter Day Saints, and she loved God. She didn't know anything about Him, but she knew He was real, that He existed. She had cried out to Him before, but this time was different. She was praying, "God, I can't take any more . . ." In despair, she opened her Bible; the pages fell open to Psalm 37, and she began to read.

Fret not thyself because of evildoers . . . for they shall soon be cut down like the grass. Rest in the Lord, and wait patiently for him; fret not thyself because of him . . . the Lord shall laugh at him; for he seeth that his day is coming . . .

As Carolyn read, a deep peace came over her, and she knew this was a message from God. Somehow, God was telling her that everything would be alright. She didn't understand the specific message, that I would be "cut down;" she only knew God had spoken to her.

Four days later, I robbed a bank. Shortly after 1:00 p.m. four days after Thanksgiving, I walked into the First National Bank on 4th street, dressed as an old man. I walked out with $9,843.00 that the government *owed* me for the seven charges from the evidence in the cigar store. In fact, I figured they still owed me $26,157.00.

I had been setting up bank robberies for years and no one who commited the robberies on my plans had ever

43

gotten caught. I'd go to a bank to check out the floor plan and get a large bill changed to see something of the arrangement of the tellers' booths. I planned the robberies shortly after 1:00 p.m. when most of the personnel were at lunch. And I chose national banks only—they were insured by the government and I was mad at the government. Not only were my plans good, but the police would never suspect me anyway. Bank robberies weren't my line of work.

Less than a month later, one day in December, FBI agents knocked on my door. I wasn't home, but Carolyn fearfully let them in to search the house. They found a can of money under the sink, and a lot more in a shoe box in Carolyn's closet. The money I had stolen was actually on its way to my bondsman for fees and to pay back the syndicate—most of the money the FBI found was from a recent poker game.

I couldn't believe they had suspected me—until I found out they had gotten a little help. Somebody had dropped the dime. I had originally planned the robbery for a friend named Sam, but he had backed out. He was on parole for bank robbery now, and he figured he would be the first one the police would suspect. I decided to go ahead and do the robbery myself; the plan was too good to waste. Sam had a girlfriend, and when the police pressured her for information about Sam, she had told them that I might know something about the robbery. She was scared, and never dreamed that I had actually done it myself. I went to Sam's house a few days later to kill him, but he had left town—in a hurry.

After the robbery and the charges, the thought kept crossing my mind that I should kill Carolyn and the children to spare them the pain if I was killed or sent to prison. If the bonds were revoked, I would be sent to prison or die fighting; my family seemed to be an albatross around my neck all the time. Things would be so easy without them. I couldn't shake the thought "get rid of *them. . . get rid of them . . .*"

That New Year's Eve, I had to drop by the house for a minute to pick something up. A man who was going to do a job for me was waiting in the car while I ran into the house. When I walked in, Carolyn thought I was home for the night, for the new year. She had stayed up, watching TV and waiting for me to come home. When she saw that I was leaving again, she couldn't hide her disappointment.

"Can't you just wait a few more minutes, until midnight?" she asked calmly. "It's almost New Year's, you know . . ."

The comment startled me. And she didn't say it in a nice way.

"I'll see you tomorrow," I grumbled as I started out the door.

Under her breath, and never intending for me to hear, she sighed, "But there may not *be* a tomorrow." I flew into a rage—just went crazy. I started shooting up the house, like I would in an act of enforcement, and kept shooting until I ran out of bullets. Mom was screaming and crying and Carolyn hid her face in her hands and sobbed. The kids huddled together under the covers in the bedroom, afraid to come out. Now was as good a time as any to get rid of all of them. I would kill Carolyn first, then Mom, then Jackie and Vern.

I threw the gun on the table and ordered Carolyn to load it. "When you finish," I shouted, "I'm going to kill you!"

Carolyn was crying uncontrollably as she picked up the gun. She knew nothing about guns and hardly knew the barrel from the trigger. With a trembling hand, she picked up the bullets and through her tears tried to load the gun. But she didn't even know where the bullets went. The pitiful sight of my wife trying to load the gun for her own

45

death only made me madder. I grabbed the gun and loaded it myself, then held it to her head. Mom was at my right elbow, crying and praying.

With tears streaming down her cheeks, Carolyn raised her eyes to meet mine and whispered, *"I love you."* I knew it wasn't a play for mercy. She knew I was a killer; she knew that once I had gone this far, I *couldn't* stop myself. I suddenly realized that she really did love me, with a love that I couldn't understand; it confused me. As I began to squeeze the trigger, something inside of me snapped, and I couldn't shoot. That had never happened before.

I spun around, stormed out of the house and shot the windows out of the new sports car I had bought for Carolyn three days earlier. I stayed away from home for a few days.

At the hearing, the FBI stacked the evidence against me—they knew they couldn't prove anything, so they just came up with a few lies. *Every* major piece of evidence they presented was a lie. They knew it and I knew it, but I couldn't call their bluff without admitting guilt.

They got what they wanted. On my son's third birthday, March 18, 1966, I was found guilty by a jury. I sent Carolyn and the children back to South Bend, in case the police tried to take me to prison. I wasn't going to prison; I'd shoot it out with the police first, and I didn't want my family around when that happened.

A few days after the hearing, I was sentenced to two 10-year prison terms. But my mouthpiece did a good job. He got the bonds set at $20,000, paid the court with syndicate money, and I was back on the bricks within minutes after sentencing. I headed back to South Bend to join my family.

When people said "Happy Jack is crazy," they meant it; they meant I was literally insane. I was no longer the happy-go-lucky kid who just loved to brawl. Something

46

new was happening inside of me and it was getting worse. It was a new kind of pain that I couldn't describe, or even name. I've never been able to describe that terrible loneliness and sense of hopelessness. I didn't care about anything, not even myself.

Off and on, I worked at a bar named "the Doghouse." It's motto was "we guarantee a fight a night and two on the weekends." If I was there, I *was* the fight. Often, I would beat guys so hard that I'd break a bone in my hand or wrist. Then I would go home and set the bones myself. Carolyn would just stare at me when I'd come home with a broken wrist.

One night, as she watched me put a cast on my wrist, she asked "Why do you do it?" I couldn't answer her. I had never really thought about it; I had never tried to figure out why I did it. I just did it. But when she asked the question, and I realized I couldn't answer her, it bothered me. Why *did* I fight? Why *did* I beat men so hard? Why *did* I enjoy violence? One night I beat a man so badly he almost died—and I didn't even mean to hurt him at all. I lost control—and I was really sick about it. He was just a guy in a bar; he wasn't an enemy; he wasn't anybody who deserved what I did to him.

I realized that I was a bomb walking around on two feet; and it didn't take much to set me off. I didn't like what I was inside, but I couldn't control it. Something was churning in the pit of my stomach all the time and I lashed out in violence at everything and everyone.

And I got even worse when I started to get paranoid. There was always the very real possibility of danger, but I saw danger where there was none. One time in a bar, a man kept staring at me, and I thought he was sizing me up for a fight. I thought he recognized me and was trying to figure if Happy Jack was really as tough as they said. The third time he stared at me, I stood up, walked over to him, tapped him on the shoulder. When he turned around. I punched him in the jaw and worked him over. I found out later that the man *had* recognized me. He thought I was somebody he knew, but he couldn't be sure so he kept staring. But far from sizing me up for a fight, he wanted to say, "hello." He was my *cousin*.

I was possessed by anger and hatred. When I woke up in the morning, I was angry. When I went to bed at night, I was angry. I hated people and I hated life itself.

But mostly, I hated myself. I have one vivid memory of that time in my life. I remember waking up one morning and walking into the bathroom. When I looked at myself in the mirror, I wanted to spit at my own face.

CHAPTER SEVEN

"You're a Dead Man. . ."

The wind against my face was cool and refreshing; the sky was full of stars, but the night was still pitch black. Not to me, though—I had smoked some high quality marijuana in a bar in Gary, and my eyes were so dilated that I could see like a cat. I was driving back to South Bend. Some drivers had been honking their horns and blinking their headlights at me, but I didn't know why—until I came to the toll booth at the exit. "Hey, buddy!" the attendant yelled, "Turn your lights on!" I had driven almost 70 miles in busy traffic without any lights.

I had been hooked on barbiturates since my time in the service, and had been smoking marijuana since I joined the syndicate. I could handle dope better than most people, but every once in a while I slipped up—like forgetting to turn my lights on. The mistakes were never very serious.

During the past year, I had tried very kind of drug in trying to find peace. I figured that something, somewhere, ought to be able to give me peace inside, and get rid of that gnawing in my heart—if I could only find it. I started taking every pill I could get my hands on and sniffing cocaine until my nose was raw.

"Hap," a friend said one night, "the only thing that will give you what you're looking for, is Horse. It's the only thing that'll do it." Horse . . . heroin.

All my life I had sworn I'd never touch heroin. It was the #1 of drugs, the king of dope. I had seen other men get on heroin and be completely destroyed in a year. A junkie couldn't even function as a good criminal; his mind was gone. I had always told myself that I would never let that happen to me—I was too professional, too good to let heroin destroy my life. But now, for the first time in my life, I wanted something that I couldn't buy, steal or get with my fists. If the king was the only thing that would give me peace, I wanted it.

I mainlined that night. I remained a heroin addict until I met another King.

Ralph Wolfe, the unorthodox cop, cropped up in my life again. We had been harrassing each other for several years, every chance we got. When Ralph was once assigned traffic duty at one of the busiest intersections in South Bend, I'd drive up quietly behind him, lay on the horn, and watch him go straight up in the air. Then I'd yell, "Just wanted to see if you were on the job, *Baby Face . . .*" Other times, I'd breeze by and yell, "Hey kid, don't you think it's time to go home—your daddy needs his uniform." He would stand in the middle of the intersection and curse me at the top of his lungs.

Another time, before the cigar store burned down, Ralph was assigned a walking beat that brought him right by my place. When I saw him coming, I would send one of my girls out to tease him. She'd invite him in for a drink—or anything else he wanted—and he would get so mad he would turn red and sputter.

But now, we weren't just two hot-headed kids any more. Over the years, the feud had become serious, and bitter,

"Happy Jack"
THE ENFORCER
. . . as he looked on October 29, 1966,
while deeply involved in a life of crime.

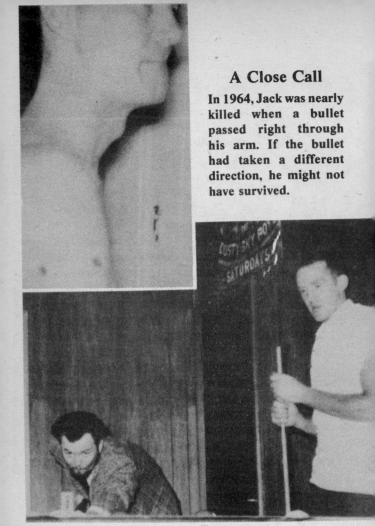

A Close Call

In 1964, Jack was nearly killed when a bullet passed right through his arm. If the bullet had taken a different direction, he might not have survived.

A Much-Feared Gangland "Enforcer"

In this 1966 photo, Jack Burbridge, at left, shoots pool with a friend, taking time out from his grim and often-violent "job assignments" as a servant of organized crime.

Charged With Armed
Bank Robbery

Jack, on the right, is handcuffed to his cousin
as they go down the hall of the Vanderburg
County, Indiana, courthouse to be arraigned
on armed bank robbery charges. This picture was taken in June, 1967.

A Deputy Sheriff and a U.S. Marshal accompany Jack as he goes to court to face sentencing in September, 1967.

Officers Take Charge of "The Enforcer"

Enroute from Indiana to New Mexico, Lt. Comdr. Howard B. Lytton, Sr. of the Indiana State Police, at right, led Jack to a saving knowledge of the Lord Jesus Christ.

The Cop And The Con

Formerly bitter adversaries, Capt. Ralph Wolfe, South Bend (Ind.) Police Department, and Jack Burbridge shake hands in the South Bend City Jail prior to the start of their "The Cop and the Con" crime prevention education programs in 1971.

Jack and His Lovely Wife, Carolyn

. . . were preparing to begin their full time
ministry for the Lord when this photograph
was taken.

Jack and Rev. Arthur Lindsay have a reunion and the opportunity to minister at the annual Christian Brotherhood Meeting at Terre Haute (Ind.) Federal Prison.

"In Prison — And Ye Visited Me"

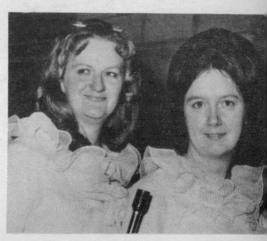

Marilyn Ford and Ruth Benson traveled with the Burridges and sang as "The Sounds of a New Life."

A Powerful Messenger Of the Lord's Saving Grace

Jack speaks at a special meeting in Melbourne, Florida. Sharing the platform with him were Singer Dave Boyer, at right, and Pastor Ed Thompson.

In churches and before businessmen's groups across the nation, Jack continues to give praise and honor to God and His mighty power by telling the amazing story of his conversion from crime to Christ.

until nothing would have pleased us more than to see the other one in a grave.

The bank in Ralph's neighborhood was robbed one afternoon, and Ralph happened to be in the drug store next door at the very moment the robbery took place. When someone ran into the drug store yelling, "the bank's been robbed!" Ralph dashed outside, only to find that patrol cars had already gathered and the robber was long gone. Ralph came unglued. "*My* bank!" he began yelling, "I know who did this! It was Happy Jack— it had to be!"

Ralph was sure I had done the robbery—and timed it deliberately to embarrass him. He could already hear the talk, how Happy Jack had really made a fool of Ralph this time. When the camera in the bank photographed a man who could have been my twin, Ralph knew beyond a shadow of a doubt that I had done it.

The FBI picked me up for questioning, but I had all kinds of proof that I hadn't committed the robbery; I had planned it, but I didn't do it myself, and the FBI let me go. That didn't stop Ralph from *knowing* I had done it. Just to nettle him, I called to tell him the good news; "Hey, Ralphie, *baby*," I sneered, "they had to let me go—you *punk* cop!" Ralph vowed then that he would get me someday. He swore that he would see me behind bars—or better yet, dead.

A few weeks later, I was sitting in the office of a used car lot, with a friend of mine, T.J., the owner. It was a sunny afternoon, but business was slow and T.J., some other men and I were lounging in the office. Suddenly, through the glass door of the office, I spotted Ralph coming through the rows of cars; he was headed straight for the office. He had a strange determined look on his face, and the men outside were egging him on. "Hey, Ralph," one guy yelled, "your old buddy's inside . . ."

51

"Yeah," Ralph answered coldly, without breaking his stride, "I see the ugly man's car."

I watched him approach. Normally, I would have been amused. But not now. Not any more. I was tired; and tired of him. And now, I was a junkie.

I've had it with that cop," I growled. "When he walks through that door, I'm going to blow him right back out." I pulled my Colt 45, rested my hand on the table in front of me and covered the gun with a newspaper. The minute Ralph opened the door, I'd pull the trigger . . . and watch the look on his face the instant he realized he had been shot!

A dead silence fell over the office; T.J. broke out in a cold sweat. No one moved a muscle as we watched Ralph coming closer and closer.

When he was a few feet from the door, I tensed, and as he grabbed the door handle, I began to squeeze the trigger. He opened the door a fraction of an inch, then hesitated. We stared at each other through the glass for an instant, then he suddenly let the door close and he quickly turned and walked away.

"Well, if that ain't the luck of a cop!" T.J. laughed nervously.

"Some luck!" I snarled, jumping up to go after him to shoot him in the back. But he had vanished; he had just disappeared.

Across the street in a coffee shop a few minutes later, T.J. told Ralph how close he had come to death. Ralph explained that as he looked at me through the door, he had seen a coldness of *death* in my eyes he had never seen before. Something had told him to move away—quickly.

I never would become a cold-blooded killer, but not because I wasn't one. Something always interfered. One day it was Carolyn. I was expecting an important phone call that day. I had told the Chicago office that my wife was always home and to leave the message, "Tell Jack it's okay," with her. When I got home that afternoon, Carolyn wasn't there and I flew into a rage. She had gone to visit her sister and hadn't been home all day. When she walked in the door, I turned her over my knee and spanked her. I was furious. It was the only time I ever hit Carolyn.

A contract was out on a man, and they wanted me to do the hit. The telephone call was an assignment to kill, and I would have accepted the job. When they couldn't get the message to me, they gave the job to somebody else.

I was still mainlining on heroin daily, but the king that was supposed to give me peace almost put me in a peaceful grave one night. J.K. and I made arrangements with a pusher to meet at the bus depot to make the transaction. The three of us arrived separately and took a table in the restaurant. The pusher promised me that the quality of his heroin was higher than the quality of street heroin. I bought a hit and went to the bathroom to shoot up. When I returned to the table, the pusher broke the news.

The quality of the heroin was fine; but he had given me enough to kill anything on two feet. "Man, you just took an O.D. You're a *dead* man . . ." He was smiling when he said it.

I didn't know, until the pusher gladly informed me, that my enemies had put a $5,000 contract out on me. The pusher had taken the job. Now, he figured death was bad enough, but *knowing* that I was going to die was an added touch of hell. He was enjoying himself.

I wasn't going to let him live to spend the $5,000—or brag that he finally wasted Happy Jack. When he stood up to leave, I pulled my gun under the table and told him to sit down.

"When I go," I growled, "you're going with me. *You're* the dead man now . . ." I didn't know it, but J.K. had done the same thing. The pusher had two guns aimed at him and if I went out before I could pull the trigger, J.K. would kill him. The pusher realized that he had made a serious mistake—a fatal one.

Within minutes, I felt myself slipping. "This is it," I thought to myself, "I'm dying . . ." I squeezed the trigger and was on the verge of shooting, when suddenly my head began to clear. In an instant, I knew I was going to make it, somehow, and a smile crossed my face. J.K. saw what was happening, and he started laughing. The pusher turned as white as a sheet and stared at me. *Nobody* could survive the overdose he had given me.

I don't remember how I got home that night. The next thing I remember was crawling up the stairs to my bedroom, calling for Carolyn to draw a hot bath for me. Carolyn jumped up and ran for a waterbottle—she thought I was having another one of my headaches and the waterbottle was the normal treatment. But when she turned on the light, she knew it wasn't a headache. I was staggering and my face was covered with flaming red blotches. She didn't know what to do, but assumed that I did. I don't know where I got the idea of a hot bath.

When I crawled into the tub, the red blotches had moved down to my chest and were still spreading. Carolyn began crying, and wanted to call my Mom, since she was a nurse. I told her she couldn't call anybody. The blotches were all over my body within minutes—and then I started tripping. At one point, I experienced the sensation of leaving my body, and being suspended above the bathroom, looking down at myself lying in the tub. I watched myself swishing water over my red body, and saw Carolyn sitting beside the tub crying her eyes out.

"Funny," I thought to myself, "I look like a lobster . . . my favorite food is lobster and I look like one . . . I am a lobster thrown into a pot of boiling water and turning red! I wonder if a lobster's wife cries like mine is when her husband is cooked . . . I am cooking . . . I am dying . . . As the tripping became more and more bizarre, a hideous laugh suddenly came out of my throat. Carolyn thought it was Satan himself; the laugh must have been blood-curdling because the young relative who was spending the night with Carolyn woke up in fright—and has been afraid of me ever since. Carolyn was terrified. She lay by the tub all night praying.

Then it was morning. The tripping gradually stopped and the redness went away. And I was left with another "gift" from my way of life—heart damage. It was a day for gifts—it was my birthday.

Two days later, the pusher died of an overdose. It was a syndicate hit to avenge his attempt on me.

I was tired. I was still strong and fast, but I was burned out. My body was wrecked and I looked like I was 49 years old, not 29. The headaches drove me out of my mind; my bones ached from all the times I had broken them; my hands were gnarled; and now on heroin, my eyes were ruined and my heart was worn out.

I didn't have much more time.

CHAPTER EIGHT

A Letter From Carolyn

Solid sheets of rain slashed across the windshield. The wipers couldn't do much against the torrential rains we hit on the outskirts of Evansville, Indiana.

Since the floor of my MG was soaked and I couldn't see to drive anyway, we'd have to stop for the night. Johnny, my cousin, a couple of girls, and I were on our way back to South Bend after a week of camping in Kentucky. Actually, I hadn't just been camping; I had been hiding.

For the past seven months, I had tried to stay out of sight; but for the past month, I had been running from the cops and the FBI. They kept coming by the house asking for me. I was wanted for questioning (and arrest) for some activities, and I knew if they ever got their hands on me this time, I'd go to prison for sure. Carolyn never knew where I was; if she had, she would have told the cops. She couldn't lie to save her life—or mine.

I had recently been awarded a promotion by the law. I was next in line for the FBI's "Most Wanted" list. The local agencies wanted me on the list, but a man had just bombed a building in Chicago, killing a lot of people. At least I wasn't a mad bomber.

Now it was late afternoon. I wanted to make it back to

South Bend that night, but I couldn't in this storm. We'd have to spend the night in Evansville.

As we checked into a motel, I'd decided that here and now was as good a time and place as any to rob a bank. I needed the money; besides, no one knew I was in town.

The next morning, I woke up late after playing pool all night. It was a hot day in July, 1967. I'd make my plans, knock over a bank, and get back to South Bend the next morning. No problem.

I contacted a man, a friend of mine I knew I could count on to shoot it out with the cops if it came to that. I told him what I had in mind. Sure, he said; he'd go along. Shortly after noon, I left the motel. I told the girls I had some business to handle and they had learned not to ask questions.

The girls, especially Ann, who had been a girlfriend for a long time, had seen the changes in me on the camping trip. I had turned into a new kind of animal on heroin, and Ann was terrified of me. She had loved me for a long time. She had been a virgin when I first met her—and turned her onto prostitution. She did it for me, to be with me. But now, I wasn't so nice to be with any more and she had to walk on eggshells around me, afraid she'd set me off. But I didn't realize how frightened of me she really was until later that day.

Shortly after 1:00 p.m., my friend and I entered a branch of the Old National Bank in Evansville. While he guarded the door, I pointed a gun at a teller, an old lady, and told her to sack it up. But I didn't scare the old hen; she glared at me and started pulling out bags of cancelled checks and dollar bills. The only problem was that I knew where the bundled money was kept—in the second drawer, and the old lady was getting the "money" from another drawer. She was trying to trick me.

"I want *money*!" I shouted, slamming my fist down on

57

the counter so hard that everyone jumped three feet. A younger teller pushed the old lady aside and started raking bundles of cash into the bags. We walked out with $13,211.

When my friend and I parted, I went back to the motel to take Ann out to eat at the motel restaurant. As we ate, we overheard a man at the next table talking about a robbery that had happened earlier that afternoon. The man was telling his friend that the police didn't have any clues; the job was too professional. The robbers couldn't be identified, the man said, because of stocking masks; in addition, they left no fingerprints. The cops had nothing to go on. Ann was listening closely to every word.

Later that day, Ann mentioned a nightclub where she wanted to go dancing that night. It was a syndicate club she had been to before. I didn't know where the club was located, but Ann said she could give me directions. She knew exactly where it was. When I was getting dressed to go, I started to put my two guns in my shoulder holster and belt, but she stopped me.

"Jack, you don't need those tonight." she said playfully. "We're just going dancing and guns will only get in the way . . ."

I threw the guns back in the suitcase and we left.

The moon was up and the night air was warm. I felt good. I was high and I had plenty of money—*their* money. Everything was working out just fine. Ann sat beside me, never speaking except to give me directions. We would go dancing, then drive back to South Bend the next morning.

"Take a right at the next intersection," Ann said. Her voice broke a little, but I didn't think anything of it. I pulled up to the intersection and swung around the corner. What I saw made my blood run cold. Immediately, in my rear view mirror, I saw two black cars pull in behind me and block the street.

The street was lined with police cars and I had driven right into the middle of them. I had never seen so many cops at one time in all my life. When I screeched to a halt, it looked like a hundred headlights came on. I was in a circle of cops. To one side were the bright lights of the TV crew and a hundred cameras flashed in the dark.

I shoved a wad of money in Ann's hands and told her to go get me a mouthpiece. I jumped out of the car and started fighting. I couldn't do anything without my guns but punch, and I punched everything that came near. I knew it was no use, but I was fighting in a blind rage. Finally, while a few cops kept me busy in front, another came up behind me and clamped a billy club under my chin. I was forced into the police car.

A few minutes later, I learned the whole story. It was a frame; *Ann* had dropped the dime. When she heard the man in the restaurant talking about the robbery, she put two and two together. At some point, she had slipped out of the motel room and called the police. The cops had told her to try to get me to a nightclub (that didn't exist) and without my guns. They gave her directions, and she had given them to me. When I found out that she, of all people, had set me up, I snapped.

The cops found the money under the bed in my motel room. I was taken to the Vanderburgh County Jail in lieu of $50,000 in bonds. There was no way, they told me, I was going to get out on bonds this time. I had been declared "a danger and menace to society" and I was going to prison this time.

I started plotting. Vanderburgh was an old jail, one that Johnny Dillinger had once broken out of. I figured it wouldn't be hard to do again. I didn't know how long I could evade the cops when I broke out. I knew I couldn't walk away this time, but for now I'd take it one step at a time. First, I had to get out. Then, I would kill Ann.

Nobody crossed me and got away with it. I hated her so much I couldn't think of anything else—not the bonds, or the money, or even prison—but getting her for this.

Four days after my arrest, I was handed a letter through the bars. It was from Carolyn. I sat down on my cot and began to read. I wasn't prepared for this.

"I have given up all hope for you," the letter began. "I have prayed for you for seven years, but now I know that not even God could reach that far down in the gutter . . . not even God could change a man like you. *I know that you will be out soon, but I don't want you to see me or the children again—ever.*"

At last, all the anger and hurt that my wife had suffered all these years had come out. When Carolyn heard that I had robbed another bank, and had been arrested, with *Ann*, she couldn't take any more. She was sick of the hurt I had caused her, sick of loneliness and fear. I didn't blame her. She had been faithful to me all these years; she had stayed with me and loved me. As I read the letter again, I realized how much she had loved me to stick it out this long.

I had pushed emotions aside for so many years. I hadn't felt the sting of rejection since I was a child. At first, I was sorry that I had lost my last tie with the outside world. But then I realized the aching in my heart was something deeper. The letter hurt me. A terrible loneliness swept over me as I sat on the cot staring at the letter. I suddenly realized that no one in the whole world *loved* me. All the times that Carolyn had nagged me, all the times she had looked at me with that hurt in her eyes, all the times she reminded me of our children—it was all because she loved me.

I had done everything a man could do to hurt his wife, and now I wanted her back. Carolyn meant every word of that letter. I had abused her love for so many years, the love was gone. No, I couldn't get her back any time soon, but maybe someday. If I could just get out of this place. I wanted more than ever to kill Ann—it was her fault that I had lost my family. She was going to pay.

Each morning, a guard came by the cells to distribute a razor blade to each prisoner; a few minutes later, he came around again to collect them. One morning, when he came to get my blade, I told him that I had dropped it down the toilet by accident. "You can come fish it out if you want to," I told him sarcastically, "but I'm sure not." He wasn't in any hurry to come into my cell, so he just shrugged and walked away.

Each weekend, a doctor came to the jail to check on prisoners who were addicts and to give the sheriff our substitute drugs for the coming week. With the razor blade I had hidden, four of us prisoners planned to take the doctor hostage.

Before I had the chance to escape, the jail officials brought me the news. Bonds had been set after all—for $150,000 this time. The syndicate was paying again. I could walk out when the paper work was done. I dropped the plans to escape and started making the arrangements.

A few days later, just before dawn, the sound of a guard outside my cell woke me up. "Burbridge," he called huskily, "get up. You're taking a trip. You're going to Albuquerque." I had to appear for a hearing there and sign the papers for bonds for the robbery there.

Half asleep, I got dressed in the dark and two guards came into my cell carrying handcuffs and shackles. It was still dark outside when I was escorted to a police car parked behind the jail in an alley. I got in the back seat, and one of the guards ran a chain around my waist, through the handcuffs, down to the shackles on my feet and finally through a hole in the floor of the car. They were taking every precaution. The guard pulled the chain tight enough

61

to allow me to get my hands to my mouth and no further.

Later that morning, the Indiana newspapers would run stories that I was still being held at the Vanderburgh jail to cover my whereabouts. The police suspected that some syndicate men might try to spring me—it would be cheaper than paying the $150,000 for me.

As the patrol car pulled out of the alley, it suddenly hit me that no one in the world knew where I was. I stared out the window into the night. Only an occasional headlight broke the darkness. I had never felt so alone.

CHAPTER NINE

That Kind of Love

Driving the police car was a U.S. Marshal. Beside him was the Lt. Commander of the Southern District of the Indiana State Police—Howard B. Lytton, Sr. I had distinguished company. I was glad the cops had to go to that much trouble for me. Since they had me, I was going to make it as miserable for them as I could.

My fists, the only solution I had known to my problems for 29 years, lay chained in my lap. If I couldn't use my hands, at least I could use my mouth and it was almost as violent as my fists anyway.

I stared at the backs of their necks. "Cops . . ." I said to myself angrily, and I started in. For the next two hours, I subjected those two cops to a steady stream of verbal garbage; I called them every foul name I knew, plus some I coined just for them. I cursed and swore at them until my jaws were tired.

The marshal tried to outswear me, but the other cop, this Mr. Lytton, just sat there. When he looked at me, he smiled. When I cursed him, he remained silent. When he spoke to me, he was polite. I couldn't remember the last time a cop was actually nice to me, but the nicer he was, the madder it made me. "*What's with this dumb cop?*" I thought to myself, "*he can't be for real . . .*"

We couldn't eat at the restaurants along the route because of my mouth. We had stopped for breakfast that morning at a restaurant, but I was so nasty to the waitress that she ran off in tears. Mr. Lytton spoke sharply to me about the incident, but he didn't raise his voice. I couldn't believe it. We ate at drive-ins the rest of the way.

And I had a lot of time to think. There was no way I could escape. The chains allowed me only enough leeway to get food to my mouth and not an inch more. I played with the handcuffs a little but I knew it was no use. I turned my attention to Ann, and thought of all the ways I could kill her. I tried to imagine the look on her face when I pulled the trigger; in my mind, I went through the scene over and over.

At about noon, and almost out of the state, we had to stop for a train. Across the flat plains, I could see the end of the train—a mile away. Suddenly a black Cadillac full of thugs pulled up behind us, and the two cops got ready to pull their guns, thinking the syndicate boys were making their move. But the thugs turned out to be just that—thugs.

When I couldn't think of any more ways to kill Ann, I started thinking about my family again. The hurt welled up inside as I remembered the letter. Carolyn's words ran through my mind over and over, "*not even God could reach that far down in the gutter . . . not even God could change a man like you . . . I don't want to see you—ever . . .*" I would get Carolyn and the children back someday, somehow.

I watched Mr. Lytton. I couldn't figure him out. Generally, he was quiet. No matter what I said to him, he was courteous. How could he be that way? What made him tick? I decided that he was for real after all. He wasn't being a phony . . . it was real.

Outside Amarillo where we were scheduled to stop for the night, the marshal and Mr. Lytton started talking about their families. When the word "family" was mentioned, Mr. Lytton lit up like a floodlight. He told the marshal all about his wife, and about how good his children were. His son, he told the marshal, was an attorney and his two daughters were school teachers. His face was beaming—there was something about his face that seemed to actually shine . . . I had never met a man like this before.

"I'm so proud of my children," he was telling the marshal.

"Well, Howard," the marshal interrupted, "I know your children must be *proud of you* for putting them through school on a policeman's salary . . . That's something I know they're *proud of you* for . . .

"*I know your children are proud of you . . . proud of you . . .* Suddenly, I remembered the words I had said to Carolyn. "*Jackie will be proud of me when she finds out her daddy is* #1 . . ." My heart felt like it was breaking in two. The words stung me now. I had been so confident, so smug. For the first time in my life I saw what kind of father I had been, what kind of man I had been. As I watched Mr. Lytton's face as he talked about his children, I realized that my children would be ashamed of me. Someday, I said to myself, I'll be like *him*; I'll get my family back and be the kind of man he is . . .

By the time we pulled up in front of the Amarillo jail, I was sick at heart. I wanted desperately to go home to Carolyn and take my children in my arms. I saw things for what they were—Mr. Lytton was sitting in the front seat of a police car, smiling, polite, a loving husband and father; *I* was sitting in the back seat of a police car wrapped in chains like a mad animal.

I was taken to a group cell, but then transferred to

solitary so that I couldn't hurt another prisoner. I slumped to my cot in despair. I had a knot in the pit of my stomach the size of a fist and a thousand thoughts and emotions were racing through my mind.

Not even God could reach that far . . . not even God . . . Carolyn's words suddenly cut into me. I tried to sleep, but I couldn't. My heart felt as though it would burst open. I saw myself beating someone in an act of enforcement. I saw scenes from my life as though they were happening right before my eyes, all the horror and violence and filth. How did my life turn out this way? I asked over and over. What was it *in* me? Why had I never before even questioned my life? How did I become so violent? What was wrong with me? Why did I have this hatred and anger? It wasn't my parents; it wasn't the law; it wasn't my enemies. It was *me.*

At last I saw the truth. It was my fault. That man—the enforcer, the pimp, the heroin addict, the bank robber— was me. I had to have a way out.

Not even God . . . As, I lay on my cot, torn up inside and in the first real agony I had ever known, I cried out to God, hoping He was real. "Oh God, if you are there, help me. If there is a God, please help me. Give me back my family! I want to be a good husband and father . . . I want to live right . . . I know I can't have my family back now, but God, if you are real, give me a hope that I can have them back. Give me a sign, before I get to Albuquerque that I can someday have them back . . . Oh *God* . . ."

But immediately, I felt a tremendous sense of guilt rise up in me. I had gone too far. All my life I had mocked God—and now I wanted His help. I had done too much. God couldn't help a man like me. No, Carolyn was right, even God couldn't reach this far down in the gutter. It was no use.

Early the next morning, I was wrapped in chains again

and we started out for the home stretch. We would be in Albuquerque that night. Maybe, I kept thinking to myself, there is a God and maybe He heard me . . . maybe. I couldn't shake off the thought. A few minutes on the road, Mr. Lytton turned to me.

"Jack," he said softly, "you're awfully quiet this morning."

"Mr. Lytton, you got to me yesterday," I answered, almost bashfully.

"Oh? I hardly said a word," he said, puzzled.

"That's partly how you got to me," I explained, "I've decided, well, I don't want to be a criminal any more. I'm hoping that somehow I can get my family back and be a good husband and father."

Mr. Lytton was like a duck hunter with a double barrelled shotgun. He almost jumped in that back seat with me.

"Jack, there's only one way," he said. And he started telling me about his friend, a man named Jesus. The light in his face when he had talked about his children was nothing compared to the way he lit up when he talked about his Friend. He started with the birth of Jesus, telling me that God loved us so much that He sent His own son to earth as a man. He told me about the way Jesus lived; he told me about the goodness, the power, the death He suffered for us on Calvary, and always, always he talked about His love. He told me that Jesus had shed His blood for me on the cross, and rose from the dead for me so that I could live. He said that Jesus wanted to come into my heart, and make me a new person; His blood could wash away all my sins . . .

My heart felt like it was on fire as Mr. Lytton talked; I was hanging on every word. It seemed that the same love he was describing was flowing out from him to me right there in that car. He wasn't lecturing me on how rotten my life had been; he was telling me why *he* lived the way he did—and how I could live the way I wanted to. But it sounded too good to be true—so maybe it wasn't true.

"Isn't that the kind of love you want?" Mr Lytton finally asked.

"Yes, it is," I answered.

"Then, let's pray," he said.

"No," I refused, "If God is real like you say, and Jesus is everything you've said He is, then He will give me that sign I asked for, that I can have my family back. Then I'll know that He really can love me."

Mr. Lytton fell into silence. I think he must have been praying the rest of the way to Albuquerque.

That afternoon, I watched the surroundings—looking for a sign. I didn't know what to expect, but I remembered from childhood that a sign was something unusual God did to prove His reality. I was ready to believe. I desperately wanted to believe, but I had dismissed Christianity as being phony for so many years. I had to *know* if Mr. Lytton was telling me the truth—or just nice words.

As we rode in silence, I searched the vast empty sky, hoping to see something unusual. I watched the farms, the cattle, the ground flying by outside the window. I wanted to see something like a bird sitting upside down on a fence. As we drew closer to Albuquerque, I decided I would settle for something less dramatic—maybe just an odd shaped cloud, or the rays of sun coming through the mountains like I had seen in inspirational paintings . . . *anything*.

But there was nothing. As we pulled up in front of Bernallio County Jail in Albuquerque, any hope I had was gone. It was over. Either God wasn't real, or else He didn't care about me. But I didn't blame him. I didn't deserve my family back.

Maybe Jesus had gone to Calvary for Mr. Lytton, but not for me. All the anger and despair came flooding back.

CHAPTER TEN

"Hey! Mr. Burbridge!"

I watched the numbers on the elevator light up. . .two . . . three . . . four . . . Mr. Lytton stood silently beside me. I knew he was hurting for me.

As we stepped out into the control center on the seventh floor, I gritted my teeth. I hated the noise, the constant hum of voices and metal. The marshall and Mr. Lytton led me to the control booth, the large oval glass office in the center of the room where prisoners were checked in and out.

The marshal handed my clothes to the sheriff in the booth, and Mr. Lytton turned to unlock my handcuffs. When he bent down to remove the shackles, I looked down at him. I had never felt such despair.

"If there is a God," I said angrily to him, "He doesn't care about me, and I don't blame Him."

When Mr. Lytton looked up at me, there was a tear in his eye. "Jack," he said slowly, "I'm going to pray for you."

"I'm praying for you, Son . . . God promised and I'm praying for you." All the hatred I had ever known rose up in me, and I wanted to hurt that cop more than I had ever wanted to hurt anybody. I tried to draw back my fist, but I

70

couldn't. I tried to kick him, but I couldn't move. "If I could just spit on him," I thought to myself, but I couldn't do that either. Inside, I had exploded, but outside, I was paralyzed.

Mr. Lytton stood up and turned toward the elevator. In one hand, he held my handcuffs and in the other my shackles. As he paused by the elevator, he looked at me one last time and he had a look of hurt in his eyes that I would never forget.

I knew that Mr. Lytton loved me. I realized then that he loved me with the same love I saw in his face when he talked about Jesus. His love hurt me and I wanted to lash out. The only person in the whole world who loves me, I thought bitterly, is a *cop.*

At that same moment, hundreds of miles away, Carolyn walked up to our bedroom; she had that hollow, empty feeling toward me. I was gone, and she was glad to be free of me. She opened her jewelry box and her eyes fell on a note that I had written to her a few months before. She had been ironing, but had to take Jackie to kindergarten; when she returned, she found the note on her ironing board, and she stuck it in her jewelry box. It read *"I love you."*

As Mr. Lytton disappeared into the elevator, the sheriff took me by the arm. I jerked away, and he backed off.

"It's okay, Jack," he said nervously, "everything's all set, and all you have to do is walk into the courtroom and sign the papers. It'll only be a matter of minutes before you're back on the bricks." He was trying to reassure me.

Suddenly, freedom didn't matter. I knew I could walk out in a few minutes, but I didn't care. The emptiness was a physical pain in my heart. Not even God cared about me, and I knew that if God didn't care about me, there was no hope for me, for my life . . . for my family.

As I turned toward the cell to dress for the hearing, the

sheriff in the control booth suddenly yelled, "Hey! Mr. Burbridge!" I turned.

"We had a phone call for you just now," the sheriff yelled, "Your family just called and your *wife* said to tell you she's praying that you will say and do the right thing in the courtroom."

Carolyn . . . At that moment, I broke inside. That sheriff might as well have yelled, "Hey, Mr. Burbridge, God is real—you see!" I went into the cell, fell on my knees and cried like a baby. I hadn't cried since I was 11 years old, but now I couldn't stop the tears. My family had called; Carolyn still loved me. God had done this —He had given me back my family—not just the sign I asked for that someday I could have them back. God did love me. Jesus did go to Calvary for me.

I didn't care that 27 other prisoners were standing in the cell watching me. Nothing mattered to me but God. My surroundings fell away, and I was a thousand miles away from the jail. I didn't know how to say a prayer. But I remembered that Mr. Lytton had told me to ask Jesus into my heart, and He would wash my sins away. I couldn't get the words out fast enough. "Jesus," I cried, "I don't know what you can do with this mess I've made of my life, but if You want it, it's Yours. Oh Jesus, come into my heart and make me a new person." As I wept and prayed, it felt like God reached down and turned a faucet on inside of me— and the hate and anger flowed out. The greatest peace I had ever known flooded my heart, and I knew something tremendous was happening to me. I poured out my heart to God—and He was pouring out His heart to me.

I don't remember how long I wept in the corner of the cell. I don't remember getting up or getting dressed. I was told later that the TV cameras filmed me as I put on my tie, but I don't remember them. Over and over the words flooded my mind, "God loves me . . . God loves me . . .

72

God loves me," and I was completely enveloped by that love. Everything else seemed unreal to me.

The next thing I remember was being escorted into the courtroom, about three hours after I had arrived at the jail. My attorney was waiting for me, but as I took my seat beside him, he seemed as foreign to me as a stranger.

"Jack, everything's all set," he whispered, patting me on the leg. "You'll be back on the bricks in a few minutes."

"Chuck, I'm not going out," I whispered back, "I'm not walking out. I'm dropping the appeals . . ."

"What kind of drug did they give you?" he exploded, "Or have you gone crazy!"

"Chuck, I have accepted Jesus as my Savior, and I can't lie any more. I robbed those banks . . ."

"You're crazy all right! You're stone cold nuts!"

Chuck hurried to the bench to talk to the judge. They whispered for a minute, and then the judge called me to the front. The judge knew that I was not a man to admit guilt. I was the type of person who was incapable of admitting guilt. I had heard a joke told about me one time that went, "If the police caught Hap running out of the bank with a bag full of money in one hand and a mask and gun in the other, he would just tell them that the robber ran by and stuck the evidence in his hand . . ."

The judge leaned over the bench, and looked at me over his glasses. "Did somebody make you a deal?" he whispered.

"No, Sir," I answered, "I accepted Jesus as my Savior. I robbed the banks and I can't lie any more . . ."

The judge looked at me, then at Chuck, then at my FBI file lying open in front of him. He sighed. "Marshal," he finally announced, "I place this man in your custody." I had confessed to the robberies, refused bonds, dropped the appeals—and the only thing the judge could do was send me to prison. I had automatically gotten myself a 20-year prison sentence—the two 10-year terms I had been given in 1966.

Reporters were standing by with their pencils poised over their notebooks. They were just looking at each other. No one could figure out what to write. No one could figure out what was happening.

Suddenly, the double doors of the courtroom swung open and in strolled Mr. Lytton. He headed for me and I headed for him, and everyone gasped. They thought we were going to attack each other. It was a "showdown" alright! Everyone in the courtroom witnessed a cop and a criminal in a bear hug, with tears rolling down our faces. We threw our arms around each other and cried. We couldn't speak. All I could do was cry, and all he could do was cry. He had gotten word that Jack Burbridge was in a corner of a cell crying and praying and Mr. Lytton knew what had happened.

Later that afternoon, the daze wore off. "What in the hell am I doing here?" I asked myself. I could have walked out and been on my way to Carolyn—scot free. "What have I done?" I asked myself over and over. I felt like I had made a complete fool of myself in front of Chuck, the judge, the press and the police. I wasn't sorry that I had turned my life over to God. Not one bit. Every time I thought of Him that strange peace welled up inside of me again. I just couldn't understand the connection between God and the courtroom. I had no objection to lying. Why had I been so pious and said I couldn't lie? I could lie and I wished I had.

At 10:30 that night, a young Mexican prisoner got up the nerve to come talk to me. The word had gotten around that I was some kind of wild man, somebody "big" since the syndicate was putting up $150,000 for me. Nobody was about to approach to ask what I thought I was doing crying and praying that afternoon. Except Lopez.

Lopez had been brought to Albuquerque from Santa Fe, where he had accepted Jesus earlier. He began to tell me about his life, about his encounter with God. He understood what had happened to me, because the same thing had happened to him. I still didn't understand it, but I appreciated Lopez for his reassurance. I felt a lot better and could finally get to sleep—and that night, for the first time in years, I slept like a baby.

The next morning, the marshal and Mr. Lytton picked me up at the jail for the trip back to Evansville—I had to plead guilty there now. All the way back, the marshal was the most uncomfortable man I had ever seen. All the way to Albuquerque, I had cursed him, and all the way to Evansville, I talked about Jesus. I was full of questions, and Mr. Lytton had all the answers. I wanted to know if my experience was real; if it would last; if I was really different, a changed man. He explained everything to me, told me why I had that deep peace inside, what had happened when I asked Jesus to come into my heart. It began to make sense.

The marshal drove like a maniac! He couldn't wait to get back to Evansville and away from me. When we finally got to Joplin, I slept in an old jail that would have been easy to escape from, because of the way the windows were made. The next morning, I told Mr. Lytton about the windows and showed him how I could have escaped. He just grinned.

When I arrived back at Vanderburgh County Jail, I wrote to Carolyn that I had "given up." She and Mom thought that I meant I had given up on life, and they jumped in the car and rushed to Evansville to talk me out of committing suicide.

When they arrived at the jail, I was taken to a small

room. The door had only two small glass windows, and Carolyn and I could only look at each other through the windows. We put our hands on the glass and cried for ten minutes. All I could say was "I'm sorry! I'm sorry!" I never had to explain to her what had happened—she knew. And Mom? She wasn't even surprised. She just said, "I knew it would happen, Son. I've been praying for you. *God promised . . .*"

As the days flew by, I knew I was different. Some mornings I would look in the mirror and almost do a double take. The features were mine, but the eyes weren't. The hatred was gone.

A week later, Carolyn brought the children to me. Jackie was now six and Vern was four years old. I was in maximum security, but the officials allowed me to visit the children without my handcuffs on for the children's sake. And I was grateful. My first brother in the Lord had been a cop, and now I was finding nice cops all around me.

Carolyn and I saw each other for the first time face to face. She searched my face for signs of the old hatred, but there was none. I loved her so much—and my children. It was as though I was really seeing them for the first time. When I took my children in my arms, my heart almost broke. God had given me these two precious lives to raise, to direct and to love, and I had failed them so miserably. I will make it all up to them, I told myself over and over.

Someday. But first, I had to go to prison. I could receive a maximum life sentence—300 years to be exact. The minimum I could receive was 45 years. It could be almost a half a century before I could even begin to be the kind of husband and father I wanted to be. But now, at least, I could be the kind of man my children would be proud of.

CHAPTER ELEVEN

Heroin and the King

Each morning when I woke up, I was afraid that I would find the old Happy Jack again. I was afraid that the deep peace would suddenly vanish overnight and I would have the familiar hatred again. But it never happened. The peace was always there. I had finally found what I had searched for all my life.

I gradually understood that I had encountered the person of Jesus Christ, the Son of the Living God, and I knew I would never be the same again. I had met Almighty God Himself, and He had done something inside of me. It was wonderful—whatever it was. It was months before I realized that I had been "saved."

As I reviewed my life, I saw the pieces fall into place. I came to realize that God had always loved me, through everything I had done. I hadn't been to church since I was a kid; I never read the Bible or associated with Christians. God was the furtherest thing from my mind. Yet, because He loved me, God had arranged my circumstances so that I *had* to associate with a Christian—trapped with Mr. Lytton in a police car.

I remembered the times that I had survived when I shouldn't have—the motorcycle accident in the Air

Force, the bomb in my car, the overdose of heroin. And Carolyn had missed the telephone call that would have made me a hit man; and I didn't have a gun the night I was arrested. It all made sense. The pieces fit together. I didn't understand *why*, but I knew that God had done it all.

I didn't miss the old life at all. I wasn't torn between the old and new Happy Jack. My attitude was "Lord, my life is *Yours*." I had made such a mess of my life that I wanted God to do whatever He could with it. I didn't think He could do anything with it. Everyone thought that my way of life was all excitement and adventure, but it wasn't. It was all pain and loneliness and emptiness. I wouldn't go back to it for anything in the world.

After a small article appeared in the newspapers, under the headline, "Bank Robber Finds God, Refuses Bonds," the trickle of Christians visiting me at Vanderburgh turned into a flood. At first, I thought they were cops, who wanted me to spill the beans on everyone I knew in the syndicate. I couldn't believe that so many strangers cared about me. When they never asked any questions I finally understood that they were Christians, wanting to give their love and support.

Some of the Christians wanted to show their love; others were trying to find out if I was for real, or if I had cleaned up my life. When one man asked me if I smoked cigarettes, I answered, "Not unless they're mary janes." His eyes got big and he hurried away in a few minutes. I was saved alright, but I still smoked marijuana and cigars, still had the temperament of a wounded alligator, with the foulest mouth on two feet and I was still a heroin addict. I thank God for the Christians who overlooked the mess my life was in, and loved me anyway.

The Gideons brought me a New Testament that would be my constant companion for years to come. I was so ignorant about God, about His Son, about the way to live.

When I began to find answers in the Bible, I knew this book was the real thing. I began to read . . . and read. I wanted to forget the past and get on with being what God wanted me to be. I hadn't been a phony before, and I wasn't going to be one now. I was only 29 years old, so I had a whole lifetime in front of me. I had lived 100% for Satan before, and I was determined to live 100% for the Lord now. I wanted to get down to business with God, and I knew I had to find out what He said, not what man thought.

When Christians gave me advice, I ran back to my cell to find it in the Bible. If the Bible didn't say it, I didn't believe it. I wanted my walk with God to be real—and I wasn't taking any chances. One day, a Christian friend said to me, "Jack, if anyone had seen you on TV fighting all those policemen when you were arrested, and then could see you sitting here now, talking about the Lord, well, no one could doubt that all things are truly possible with God!"

When he left, I went back to my cell and looked it up. There it was, in the Bible—"With God, *all* things are possible." What the man had said was true. If God could change my heart, I reasoned, then He could take care of my heroin addiction . . .

A guard distributed substitute drugs three times a day to the prisoners with drug habits. That afternoon, he came to my cell as usual.

"Here, Burbridge," he said, handing the cup through the bars.

"I don't want any more," I said bravely, "I'm not taking any more drugs."

"Oh, yeah?" he answered sarcastically, "Well, by tomorrow morning, you'll be ready for 'em."

I had seen people go through heroin withdrawal and it wasn't a pretty sight. At best, it took three days and nights of sheer hell; at worst, the addict died. God wasn't going to let anything happen to me—after all, "With God, all things are possible."

By midnight, I thought I was dying. I lay on my cot in agony and wished I *could* die. Every muscle in my body ached, every bone felt like it was on fire. My vision blurred and I was hot and cold at the same time. The pain was different from anything I had ever known. And I thought I had made a big mistake. Maybe all things weren't possible with God after all. Maybe God wanted me to sweat it out alone.

I opened my Bible and tried to read, but I couldn't even focus on the page, much less the words. I closed it and held it to my chest. Just then, the sheriff walked by and saw me, clutching my Bible.

"Hey, Burbridge," he sneered, "You might as well throw that thing away. It's not going to do you any good now. Like I told you before, religion is only for women, children and sissies."

He had told me that before, and I had always answered, "Well, I'm obviously no woman. I'm not a child because I'm almost 30 years old. And if you think I'm a sissy, step in here and find out what kind of sissy I am . . ." But tonight, I was too sick to answer. The sheriff walked away, laughing.

"Lord," I prayed silently, "That man needs You. Touch him, Lord, like You touched me. Lord . . ." Then I passed out. I didn't go to sleep; I lost consciousness.

Then it was morning. I opened my eyes and stared at the ceiling for a moment, trying to decide if I was still alive. It felt like I *wasn't*, so I jumped out of bed. I was fine, but my room looked like a tornado had come through. The mattress was soaking wet and yellow with perspiration. The pillow was on the floor, and my blanket was crumpled in a heap in the far corner.

But I was *clean.* My body hadn't felt so good since I was a kid. I knew immediately what had happened. I hadn't been through withdrawal; I had been *healed.* God had knocked me out and healed me during the night—and I had slept through it. I was so excited that I wanted to do cartwheels.

Then I heard the sheriff coming. Usually, when he made his morning rounds, he raised any racket he could—whistling, banging on the doors, rattling his keys. But this morning, he was tiptoeing. He had seen what was going on in my cell during the night, and he figured I would be some kind of animal this morning.

As he came around the corner to peek into my cell, I yelled, "Praise the Lord!" and it startled him so much that he almost dropped his tray. He studied me for a minute. Even on the substitutes, I should have been shaking like a leaf.

"One of those so-called Christians slipped you a fix!" he finally said.

"No!" I answered excitedly, "*Jesus* touched me . . ."

He flew downstairs. In a minute, he came flying back up with another official. They searched every inch of my cell, and made me strip to look for fresh needle marks. They were sure a "Christian" had supplied me with heroin. They took me to the bullpen in front of the sergeant's desk downstairs.

"Don't give this man any coffee, bathroom privileges or anything," the sheriff ordered the sergeant. "He got some junk last night and we're gonna find out how."

About two hours later, the doctor came. He was as determined as the sheriff. But I was getting happier by the minute. The doctor took blood and urine samples and examined my body for fresh needle marks.

"We're not only going to find out what you got," he

81

said, looking me straight in the eye, "but we're even going to tell you what percent you got . . ."

"Doc," I answered, "The only thing you're going to find in me is the pure clean blood of Jesus . . ."

"Boy, are you ever wired up!" one guard said, winking at the doctor.

"He really got some good junk last night!" the sheriff laughed.

The doctor hurried away to run tests on the samples. Hours later, he came back. He didn't look too happy.

"Couldn't find anything, could you Doc?" I asked, grinning. He wouldn't answer. He just stared at me. When the sheriff walked up to us, the doctor, without taking his eyes off me, handed him a little slip of yellow paper.

"It's one of those phenomenal things that happens every once in a while," the doctor said slowly. "*He is clean. There's not even a trace of the substitute in his blood stream.*"

I wanted to shout. Instead, I said, "I tried to tell you, Doc!" That slip of little paper became a permanent part of my prison records—a testimony to the power of God.

Two days later, I was sitting in the bullpen reading in my Bible where the Apostle Paul wrote that we should live Christ-like. "Yeah, that's right," I thought to myself as I reached for a Dutch Masters, "We *should* live Christ-like." I kept reading, licked my cigar up, and lit it. It didn't taste very good. Every once in a while the cigar wrapper has a hole in it and the tobacco gets stale—that must be the problem, I told myself. I started to put it out, when the guy across the table from me, yelled, "Hey, man!" Don't do that! If you don't want it, give it to me." I handed it to him, and watched him puff away. It smelled okay; in fact, when he started blowing that blue smoke in my face, it smelled wonderful.

I went back to my cell and got another cigar. I got it wet

and put the fire to it. But it tasted as bad as the first one. "*Two* bum cigars in one box!" I thought to myself, annoyed. "That's ridiculous!" I pulled the cigar out of my mouth and stared at it. The guy across the table was still puffing away on the first one.

"*My taste buds are ruined.* That must be it," I told myself. "Now that I'm off drugs, nothing will ever taste good to me again." But then, suddenly, the Lord brought the words back to me—I should live Christ-like— and I realized what that meant. I couldn't picture Jesus walking down the streets of Jerusalem with a big, fat, Dutch Masters in His mouth.

I went back to my cell and came back with the whole box. "Here," I said to my friend across the table, "You can have them all." He was overwhelmed with gratitude. He thought I was crazy, but he was grateful.

I understood what God was doing. I had come to Him like an orphan—poor, homeless, hungry and caked with mud. He had taken me in, brought me to the feast, given me all that He had—and now He was cleaning me up. I was praying, "Go ahead, Lord!" The only problem was that after the heroin and the cigars, I thought I *was* clean. What else was there? I gave all the credit to Jesus. I would tell anybody, any time, any place that Jesus had done it all, and if a guy didn't believe me, I would punch him—or curse him like a sailor.

One night, I was reading my Gideon's Bible again, when two guys started banging on a table in the bullpen, near my cell. I got up and went out to them.

"Hey, guys," I said politely, "Would you mind quieting down? I'm trying to read my Bible."

"Hey! Listen to that!" one guy mocked. "Hap says he's trying to read his *Bible*! That's pretty good, Hap" The other guy rocked with laughter.

Before I knew what I was doing, I caught one guy under

83

the chin with my right fist and he landed under the table. I wheeled around to the other guy, but he was backing away as fast as he could walk backwards. He backed into a corner and threw up his hands.

"Hap, I didn't do it!" he said frantically, "He did it! I stopped when you told me to! We just thought you were joking!"

Everybody at Vanderburgh thought I was joking. So instead of hitting the guy, I just gave him my best kind of tongue-lashing. I cursed him with every name in the book.

I went back to my cell and opened my Bible again. As soon as my eyes fell on the page, I realized what I had done, and I was sick at heart. All the foul names ran through my mind, and I realized what the words actually meant. And about 95% of them involved the name of Jesus. I felt worse than I had at any time since I had been saved, and I got down on my knees and cried. "Lord, I'd rather have You cut my tongue out than to let me use Your name like that!" I vowed that I would never use His name in cursing again.

After that, I lost half my vocabulary. I had to learn to talk all over again. I would open my mouth to talk—then have to shut it until I could think of *nice* words. I realized then that I didn't have my tongue—my tongue had me. My mouth had been obscene, but I wasn't aware of it until I tried to talk without the filth.

I had been at Vanderburgh for six weeks now. The time had passed rapidly, and I was happier than I had ever dreamed I could be. Day by day, Jesus became more real to me, and the man I had once been grew dimmer and dimmer.

Now, the day of sentencing arrived. I had 20 years already for the Albuquerque robbery, and it was only a question of how many more years I would get for the

Evansville robbery. I could get a total of 45 years for both robberies; I tried not to think about it.

I knew I had to go to prison; it was what the Lord wanted. I figured pulling time would be good for my witness, so guys couldn't say, "Yeah, it was easy for you to be a Christian—you were on the outside." I thought God was through with me, and from then on I'd just be marking time. But He had more in mind for me—a lot more.

CHAPTER TWELVE

Judgment Day

Today was judgment day. I thought I was strong inside. I thought I could face it. I thought I was so spiritual that I had even made a covenant with God to witness to at least one man every day of every year I received—even if it was the rest of my life.

I was handcuffed to a policeman on each side and we began the walk to the courtroom down the street—the longest walk I had ever made. When I stepped off the last stair onto the alley, I thought I was sinking. It suddenly struck me how long 45 years really was. I would be 75 years old when I got out of prison! My life would be over. I broke inside, and my heart turned to jelly. I had never been so afraid in my whole life.

The press crowded in around us, and I felt as though I was walking to my death. *This must be what it is like*, I thought to myself, *to walk to the gas chamber.* I tried to remember that I had given my life to Jesus, and only wanted to serve Him the rest of my life. I tried to remember that it wasn't *my* life any more, that I belonged to Him. But nothing helped. I couldn't think of anything but those 45 years.

Mom and Carolyn were already seated in the courtroom when I was escorted in. Our eyes met for a moment before I was taken to the front. They would be going home after the hearing; I might not be able to join them for 45 years.

My heart sank as the Honorable James E. Noland took his place at the bench. He had a reputation as a real "hanging judge" and he *looked* like one. I cringed as he opened my FBI file—that was now 2½ inches thick—in front of him. Jesus had taken my life and turned it upside down six weeks earlier, but to the judicial system, I was still, "Jack A. Burbridge . . . "Happy Jack" . . . Organized Crime; EXTREMELY DANGEROUS; arrested—gun smuggling, prostitution, drugs, bank robbery . . ."

I listened to the U.S. attorney spend almost two hours telling Judge Noland why I should receive the full 45 years in prison. The longer he talked, the lower I sank. By the time he finished, I wanted to crawl under the table. It seemed like he brought up almost every act of violence I had ever committed, and described the violence, the criminal activities and the robberies in vivid detail. I could see the disgust on Judge Noland's face.

When my attorney got his turn, he asked for mercy on two counts—my wonderful wife and children; and my honorable discharge from the Air Force. He didn't even bother to deny that I was the monster the U.S. attorney claimed. His defense only made me feel worse—I didn't deserve mercy as a family man or a soldier.

Finally, Judge Noland called me to the bench. When I stood up, my legs turned to rubber bands. When I finally made it to the bench, I thought I would fall down any minute. I was so desperate that I couldn't pray, but I began to repeat the name of Jesus. Over and over, I silently cried, "Jesus . . . Jesus . . . Jesus . . ." In a moment, I felt strength flow into my body, and it was as though Jesus walked into

87

the courtroom. His presence was so strong that I wouldn't have been surprised to turn around and see Him standing at the door. I wasn't the only one who felt Him either. People all over the room, most of them perfect strangers, began to weep.

The judge glared at me and started telling me exactly what he thought of me. He almost spit the words at me. He told me that I was the type of person who had made crime a profession. I hadn't ended up as a criminal by accident, or by a few mistakes. I had deliberately become a career criminal. He told me that I was a detriment to society and deserved everything he could give me. Suddenly, I was thankful that he couldn't give me the electric chair. He wanted to put me out of my misery, he explained, and do the whole world a favor. But I just kept repeating the name of Jesus.

Finally, he announced the sentence. The two 10-year terms for the Albuquerque robbery would run concurrently. That made 10 years. Then I would serve 12 years for the Evansville robbery. My total sentence was 22 years—only two years more than I had when I came into court!

I returned to my seat and started crying. Silently, I praised God for His mercy. I couldn't believe the sentence—it was less than *half* the minimum I should have received. The judge called a young felon and sentenced him to a year and a day in the pen; the young man started cursing and wouldn't stop until Judge Noland threatened him with contempt of court. The guy took his seat near me, still grumbling and cursing. *I* was still smiling and praising God. Every once in a while, he glanced over at me.

"I don't have to go to prison with him, do I?" the young man finally asked the marshal.

"Well, yes. Why?" the marshal answered.

"He's crazy" the young man whispered. "Anybody who's happy over a 22-year sentence has got to be crazy—plum nuts!"

Suddenly, Judge Noland called me back to the bench. A hush fell over the courtroom. For the first time in the history of the U.S. District Court, a man was called back for re-sentencing. My heart sank to my shoes. There had been a mistake. My sentence would be *32* years, not 22—I just knew it. The judge had made a slip of the tongue.

"Burbridge," Judge Noland said, "the sentence does not read the way I want it to." My heart pounded against my chest.

"It will be a composite sentence," Judge Noland continued, "of 12 years under 42-8A."

Twelve years? Was it possible that he had reduced my sentence to 12 years? I began crying again.

"Burbridge," Judge Noland asked, "Do you know what a 42-8A means?"

"No sir," I answered through my tears, "not unless it means that I will serve all of it." I was *happy* to serve all of 12 years!

"No," he answered sharply, "it means that you are eligible for parole immediately by the jurisdiction of the United States parole board."

Twelve years and eligible for parole? I couldn't believe my ears. I had eight years less than when I had come to the hearing. I knew that Jesus had walked into that courtroom, and I wanted to fall at His feet.

When the court was adjourned a few minutes later, I tried to get permission to see Judge Noland. I wanted to thank him. But he refused to see me. He had had every intention of giving me the full 45 years and now, I figured, he couldn't understand why he had given me such a light sentence. I found out later that far from being a "hanging judge," he was a *"praying* judge;" he had prayed that morning before court that he would do God's will.

The U.S. attorney and the FBI were shocked and furious over my sentence. To them, it was just another example of judges being too easy on "professional" criminals.

I was taken to a cage-like structure in a room adjoining the courtroom and given a few precious minutes with Carolyn and Mom. As we rejoiced together, the marshal walked over to us.

"We don't know what happened, Burbridge," he said, "But you must have gotten to somebody . . ." He rubbed his fingers together, implying that I had paid off the judge.

Mom, Carolyn and I together pointed toward Heaven and said, "We did get to Somebody—to the *Lord* through prayer."

We discovered a short time later that the 42-8A classification for paroles was adopted only shortly before my sentencing.

A few days after the hearing, the marshal and Mr. Lytton came for me at Vanderburgh early one morning. It was time to go. As we drove to the penitentiary where I would spend the next 12 years of my life, Mr. Lytton and I rejoiced together.

That afternoon, we drove into the red sprawling complex of Terre Haute in southern Indiana. My heart was pounding as I stared at the severe red brick buildings surrounded by 18 foot fences laced with barbed wire.

When the paperwork was finished, I said good-bye to Mr. Lytton. I thanked him over and over again for all he had done for me. We shook hands and he left.

As he opened the door, he turned to look at me once more, and I remembered another time he had done that . . . an eternity ago. But now he was smiling as he disappeared through the door.

CHAPTER THIRTEEN

Happy Jack, the Preacher

"Burbridge, your angle won't work here," a rough-looking official with piercing gray eyes barked. My "angle," of course, was using religion to get out on parole.

"You may be eligible for parole," he continued, "but as far as we're concerned, you got your parole in the courtroom. It's up to us now . . ."

If I worked in "industries," however, I could earn two days a month good time for the first year, then four days a month after that. In addition, the official explained, I would be paid 17 cents an hour.

It wasn't exactly the income I was accustomed to, but at least I could send the money home to Carolyn. I told the official to sign me up for a job and I was assigned as a time-study keeper and payroll accountant—probably because of my "banking experience."

It was my first day at Terre Haute, and I was given a "welcoming party" that afternoon in the A & O Cell (Admissions and Orientation) by some of my old friends. They presented me with coffee, tea and cigars, since I hadn't had time to go to the commissary. Knowing me as they did, they figured I'd have a cigar stuck in my mouth all the time for 12 years. I didn't tell them that cigar smoke made me sick to my stomach now!

I matter-of-factly told the guys what had happened to me, and they said, "Yeah, Hap, that's a good angle. That's just fine, but with your temperament, you'll never make it. You'll last five or six months, then you'll kill some sucker." Everybody in prison "shoots an angle," and they figured religion was as good or better than most—if I could keep it up. They accepted me as an old buddy and wished me luck.

I made myself at home in a 6' by 10' maximum security cell, cell 64, cell block D, second range. I put on my dead blue uniform and stuck the Gideon's Bible in my pocket.

I had friends in Terre Haute, but I had enemies too—some professional killers, some just out for revenge because of something I had done to them once. It was easy to walk up behind a man in the hall, stick a shank in his back and walk away. It happened often. I had to trust the Lord—He was the only person who could be trusted—to preserve my life. If He wanted to take my life, that was okay with me.

"Drink a lot of water and walk slow," was the way to get along in the joint. The water kept the kidneys flushed out and nobody hurried because there was no place to go.

The adjustment to prison life wasn't difficult for me; I just thought of myself as pulling time like a lot of other guys. I dug in, tried to behave myself. I wanted to stay active so I wouldn't get soft, so I usually did 100 pushups a day. Soon, I was designing cars, selling some art work in the prison art shows, and trying to do my part in prison reform. I never had believed in wasting time, and in 12 years I could accomplish a lot if I stayed busy.

I chalked off the days like everyone else. Carolyn and I were allowed 10 hours a month to visit, and she came whenever she could, usually one weekend. A few days before and after her visit, I pulled "hard time." It was hard to know that she was coming; then have to turn my back and walk away from her.

I hadn't been in Terre Haute long before I began having terrible nightmares. They were always the same—scenes from my old way of life. I knew that I was forgiven. I knew that the slate was clean. In fact, during the day time, I didn't think about my old life. But as soon as my head hit the pillow at night, horrible scenes, from true life, began flashing through my mind. Afterwards, I tossed and turned, plagued by guilt of what I had done to so many people.

When I went to sleep, I re-lived, detail by detail, some experience from my life. And the dreams were so vivid that my body would almost be acting out the scenes. If I dreamed I was running after a shoot out, I woke up sweating, and my leg muscles would be tense. If I dreamed of an act of enforcement, I woke up with clenched fists. Sometimes I dreamed of violence, or sex, or drugs. But mostly, I would see myself beating someone over and over, and hear the screams and see the blood on his face and my hands. It was sheer hell.

I would wake up with a start during these nightmares, and sigh with relief that it was only a dream. But the guilt I felt when I re-lived those actions when I was so brutal was more than I could bear. I couldn't understand why I was still experiencing such guilt.

Finally, after a few weeks of nightmares almost every night, I had an especially vivid dream. It was of an actual experience, once again, from an act of enforcement. I woke up in a pool of sweat, and felt tormented. I couldn't go on like this; I'd lose my mind. I cried out, "God, am I forgiven? Oh Lord, am I really forgiven?" I reached for my Bible, and my eyes fell on Matthew 12:31. I read that "all manner of sin" was forgiven me, *except* blasphemy against the Holy Spirit. I thought about that for a moment. I had committed all manner of sin—but I had never spoken a word against the Holy Spirit! The "light" came on in my mind, and I suddenly knew that I had been forgiven. I had known it before in my head, but now I knew it in my heart. I had a spotless record with God. I was as clean as if I had been a Christian all my life.

If the nightmares weren't from God, and they weren't from me, they could only be from one other source. I jumped out of bed and started rebuking Satan and ordering him out of my cell. Just to be safe, I ordered old Slewfoot out of my bed, off my pillow, off my walls, out of my coffee pot, off my locker, out of the light fixture and everything else I could point a finger at in my cell. I had a great time. If a guard had come along, he surely would have thought I had gone mad!

From that night on, I never had another nightmare.

I joined a group named "The Christian Brotherhood," that met for fellowship. At first, there were only a few of us. Then the Lord began transferring other Christians to Terre Haute and soon I had several close Christian friends. Seven of us who wanted to get serious with the Lord formed a prayer and Bible study group, and began to seek what we called "the fullness of the Lord." We didn't know what that was, but we wanted the power of God to move at Terre Haute in His "fullness."

Terre Haute was the mid-western penitentiary where troublemakers from other prisons were sent. Leavenworth, in Kansas, had the reputation of being the worst (most dangerous) prison, but officials and other prisons said Terre Haute was just as bad, even though it was smaller. In short, the men at Terre Haute were mostly hard-core criminals, the tough characters in crime. The men in our prayer group wanted the Lord to move at Terre Haute; some of us had been cold-blooded killers, but most of that type of men at Terre Haute knew nothing about the gospel. I knew if God could change a man like me, He could change anybody. The brothers and I had been in the middle of the action before we were saved, and we still wanted to be in the middle of the action now—God's action. We knew it would take the power of God shaking Terre Haute in a tremendous revival to reach the men at Terre Haute. At the moment, nothing was happening.

I wasn't helping much, to be honest. I hadn't forgotten my covenant with God, to witness to at least one man every day of my sentence. Twelve years gave me 4,382 days (including a couple of leap years) to witness to 1,127 men. I started witnessing, and all it got me was a smart mouth. I was talking about Jesus and carrying my Bible, and it wasn't long before I was called, "Bible-toter," or "reverend." It made me furious—and I mean *furious*. All I was doing was making a mess of things, witnessing, quoting Scripture and punching guys out. As it turned out, the struggle over my temper (and fists) was the hardest I had had. Violence had been my life for 30 years.

The brothers in the prayer group began to read about the power of prayer and fasting in the Bible. The longer we prayed about it, the stronger we felt that we should fast for the power of God to fall at Terre Haute. We weren't Christians who did things halfheartedly, so we chose to fast in a big way —40 days.

The first few days were rough, but gradually, with each passing day, the gnawing in my stomach subsided. After a week, it wasn't any problem; my appetite was gone. I was shedding pounds faster than I could count. I had been tall and lean; now I was tall and skinny.

On the 27th day of our fast, we were called into the associate warden's office. He had noticed that seven men had suddenly stopped eating and were getting awfully thin.

"It's not going to work," he began solemnly when we

arrived in his office. "You're not going through with this."

We were puzzled and asked what he meant.

"You're not going through with this hunger strike," he answered grimly, "You'll never get skinny enough to slip through the bars."

We had to laugh. We explained to him that we weren't on a hunger strike, but were fasting for a revival at Terre Haute.

"You mean a *church*-type revival?" It was his turn to laugh. He decided that we were harmless enough, but he still ordered us to eat one meal a day. We chose breakfast since it was the lightest meal of the day.

But that made it even harder. It was the hardest thing I had ever done. The food at breakfast "confused" the stomach, so it kept operating, instead of closing down like it was supposed to. My appetite came back to stay, and each day was like starting the fast all over again. In addition, since we were eating one meal, we decided we should fast longer, and we extended the fast another three months. We stuck to it and trusted the Lord to bless us.

One day, the fast kept us out of a riot in the chow hall. Some trouble started with a few guys and soon the whole prison was rioting. As a result, a shake-down occurred. Prisoners were transferred out, the institution was on deadlock (no prisoners in or out), and some inmates were put in the hole. But my brothers and I were in the chapel, praying, everyone knew it.

Before each meal, the prison's Catholic chaplain conducted a mass, and the men who were fasting attended. We learned the responses, and when the Catholics said rosary, we just prayed—all of us in the prayer group were Protestant. One day, we arrived at mass to find a new chaplain, who didn't know us or the Brotherhood. We continued attending mass as usual, and one day, after mass the chaplain called us aside.

"I've got something for you men," he said to us cheerfully. "I've noticed that none of you have rosaries, so I got some for you." He held out several little plastic bags of rosaries.

"Chaplain, we appreciate this," Rocky, one of the brothers, said, laughing, "But we're not Catholics!"

"What do you mean you're not Catholics!" he exclaimed, "You're the best Catholics I've got! You don't miss a mass!"

We explained to him about the Brotherhood, the prayer group and the fast. He was so impressed that he joined us. Little by little, the group was growing. Now, it had almost 30 members.

I was still struggling with my temper. It was a daily fight to keep from hitting somebody. I finally learned to rush back to my cell and *sit* on my hands when somebody made me mad. One day, when I was about to explode, I went to my cell and opened my Bible; my eyes fell on the words of Jesus, when He told His disciples to rejoice when they were persecuted and "reviled" for His sake because they were gaining in glory and their reward would be great. I was definitely being "reviled." Hallelujah! I thought to myself. After that, when someone yelled, "Hey preacher!" I yelled back, "Why, God bless you! I don't deserve a title like that!" or "Thank you brother! Lord, don't stop them now, I need all the glory I can get!" Then *he* and not me, would end up getting mad.

Finally, I made it almost six weeks without hitting anybody. I thought I was doing fine. I thought I had conquered my fists. I *thought*.

One day four prisoners were sitting around a table in the day room area, and two of them were homosexuals. I didn't go in for that kind of thing at all. When I walked by them, one of the gays made a remark.

97

"Been to another prayer meeting?" he asked sarcastically.

"Yes, as a matter of fact, I have . . ." So far so good.

"You know," another man broke in, "I figure Jesus must have been a queer—the only people He ever associated with were men . . ."

Before I knew what was happening, I had the guy around the neck, gripping his head under my arm and was running him toward a concrete pillar in the room. I was going to flatten his head against it. In a second, I realized what I was doing, and I let him go immediately. But we were moving so fast he still ran into the column, and I had to run past it before I could stop.

"Man, I'm sorry! I'm really sorry!" I apologized to him, "God doesn't want me to act like this! I'm sorry."

"No, man, *I'm* sorry," he said, "I was just joking. I didn't mean anything by what I said."

"No," I insisted, "Forgive me."

I went back to my cell and fell on my knees. I remembered the words of my old friend, "Hap, you'll last five or six months, then you'll kill . . ." I had wanted to kill that man; I had wanted to spill his brains against the pillar. I was that mad. But what scared me was that it had happened so fast—it was that same split-second reaction that had kept me *alive* for 30 years. I prayed that day with all my heart. I had to control my temper, or I would kill somebody someday, and then everyone would say, "Sorry, Hap, you blew it; we told you that you wouldn't make it. It was a good angle, though. Too bad you couldn't make it."

After that day, I still had flare-ups inside and sometimes I'd fume deep down inside; but I never hit anybody again.

Before I realized it, a year had passed. I was a different man from the one who first came to Terre Haute. For one thing, I had lived in the Word of God. When I first came, I

98

hardly knew Genesis from Corinthians; now, I not only knew the scriptures, but I knew where to find individual scriptures. God spoke to me often through His Word, showing me faults and problems I still had, but also showing me His reality and the reality of what He had done for me. I knew that I would never go back to my old way of life. I had come too far and was too happy. There was nothing that could have tempted me to trade one day with Jesus for all the money and power I might have had before that day in Albuquerque.

But still, the excitement was wearing off. I wanted to get more and more excited, not less! The "fullness of the Lord" was definitely missing. Where was the joy unspeakable that the Bible spoke of? Where were the rivers of living waters flowing out of me that Jesus had promised?

We had prayed and fasted that the Lord would send a mighty revival to Terre Haute. It was about to begin, but we never dreamed it would begin with us.

CHAPTER FOURTEEN

The Fullness of the Lord

Of all the preachers and laymen who came to visit the men at Terre Haute, there was one man who stood out.

His name was Arthur Lindsey, a little fireball who came to prison twice a week at his own time and expense. He was a dynamo, flying around the halls about three feet off the ground, teaching, preaching and praying with the men. He radiated joy all the time. He was *on fire*.

One night after a Brotherhood meeting, I approached Mr. Lindsey.

"Brother Lindsey," I began, "What is it that you've got that other preachers don't have?"

Without a moment's hesitation, he blurted out, "It's the Holy Ghost, Jack! Just read the book of Acts."

I did read the book of Acts, over and over. I read that Jesus told His disciples to wait in Jerusalem until the Holy Spirit came. They weren't supposed to witness or preach or teach until they received the Holy Spirit; then, and only then, according to the scriptures, would they have power. I read that after the Spirit came, the disciples turned their world upside down. Peter preached to 3,000 people that day and every last one of them was saved. I read about all the miracles the disciples did by the Spirit. By the time I finished reading Acts the second time, I wanted this Acts power. "Jack," I told myself, "This is it. This is exactly what you need; this is that 'fullness of the Lord' you've been praying for!"

When Mr. Lindsey came back to the prison, I asked him how I could get this power of God. He grinned and quoted to me, "Seek ye first the kingdom of God and His righteousness, and *all* these things shall be added unto you."

"Just seek Jesus," he emphasized, "and don't seek the filling of the Holy Ghost. Ask for more of Jesus. Then you'll get the power.

I rushed back to my cell, got on my knees, and prayed, "Lord, I want more of you. I love you, Lord Jesus . . . now please fill me with the Holy Spirit.

For months, one particular guard had been harrassing me every chance he got. He had a chip the size of a log on his shoulder, and he tried everything he could to make my life miserable.

One day, the guard called me over to him. In his hand, he held my "idiot card," a 5"x 8" card with my mug shot and a brief description of my criminal activities. Following my name were the initials "O.C." for "organized crime"; then EXTREMELY VIOLENT in big red letters.

"You Jack Burbridge?" the guard grumbled, looking at my idiot card, then at me.

"Yes Sir."

"You don't look 'extremely violent' to me."

I knew it was a challenge. "Well, Sir, I'm not."

"You callin' the institution a liar, *boy*. . .?" he barked. I could feel the anger rise up in me.

"No Sir," I answered calmly, "It's just that the institution is going by my past life, not by the way I am now. On July 28, 1967, I accepted Jesus as my Saviour, and He changed my life. I'm not extremely violent any more."

He stared at me a minute, and then said, "Oh yeah? We'll see about that." He walked away. I knew what was coming.

Every day, the guard tore up my cell. Officially, it was a "shake-down." He could do it any time to look for drugs or weapons; but we both knew what he wanted—for me to break.

Every afternoon when I returned to my cell after work, I found my cell in a wreck. My Bible studies were scattered all over the floor, and my cot was torn apart. In addition, my instant orange juice and coffee were emptied on top of my locker.

Even worse, the guard stood on the range outside my door just to watch my reaction. I would swing the door open and yell, "Praise the Lord! Now I have something to do for the next couple of hours!" That was for his benefit. When he left, I got on my knees and told the Lord the truth—I wanted to punch that guard in the jaw, and someday I might just do it.

One day, a memorandum was issued, forbidding the men to hang pin-up pictures on their cell walls. The situation had gotten out of hand. Some men had so many girly pictures on their walls that the cells looked like they had been wallpapered.

I had one picture on my wall. It was a picture of Jesus. My family had sent it to me as a gift. In this painting, He had such a look of compassion on His face, and I received strength from it. Everytime I looked at the picture, I remembered that Jesus had lived as a man of flesh and blood, and He, too, had once been in prison. And He was even beaten by His guards.

The day the memo was issued, I went to my cell after work, expecting to find the usual mess. But there was something new—my picture of Jesus was lying in the middle of my cot—torn into six pieces. It was more than I could handle. I fell on my knees and cried, "Jesus, You've got to do something. You promised you wouldn't give me more than I could bear and I can't bear any more!"

Two days later, the guard was transferred to the night shift, and didn't shake my cell down any more. He wouldn't have an excuse to. He couldn't have justified a nightly shake-down when he could see that the prisoner was sound asleep. I praised God for the relief from the guard. But it wasn't long before he began harrassing me again.

From 11 p.m. to 7 a.m. was lights-out time all over the prison. That was the time that I really contacted the Lord. I had learned early that I couldn't really get in close touch with Him in books or tapes or any other Christian material, no matter how good they were. I had to find Him on my knees in deep prayer.

The guard always came to my cell to check on me. If a guard wanted to see if a prisoner was behaving himself, he would make a noise at the door until he got a response. That night, the guard pecked on my door with a key and shined his flashlight through the small glass window. He could see that I wasn't in the middle of digging my way out of Terre Haute, but he kept pecking. Finally, I threw my hands in the air and yelled "Okay!"

Once again I was angry. I could see that no matter what shift that guard was on, he was determined to keep pounding at me. Only God could help—by touching the guard. I cried out to God to save the guard. "Oh Lord," I prayed, "Please do something about that man—he's in a worse prison that I am. He must be a miserable man . . ." The Lord did do something—but not to the guard!

From way deep inside of me, something started to churn. A heavy sensation came over me and flowed inside of me. I wasn't sure what was happening, but I had a pretty good idea! I realized that the Lord was pouring out His Spirit upon me. The room was filled with the presence of

God and my body felt electrified. I stayed on my knees for hours and hours. I never wanted to stop. I knew that I was in the very presence of Almighty God.

I don't remember going to sleep that night, but when I woke up, I couldn't wait to tell my brothers in the prayer group about the fullness of the Lord we had been praying for.

I sailed across the range and down the steps. Suddenly, I heard, "Hey, reverend!" It was the guard. But this morning, I was too excited to get mad.

"Come here," he ordered. I went to him.

"You *sick* last night or somethin'?" he sneered.

"No sir, I got filled with the Holy Spirit!"

The guard's eyes got big and he turned as white as a sheet. He hurried away as fast as he could. From that day on, he didn't touch my cell; in fact, he stayed as far away from me as he could. The only thing he ever called me for the rest of my time in Terre Haute was "Burbridge, 25012-138!"

I rushed to the chow hall to break the news to the brothers. They weren't as excited as I thought they'd be. They told me I had gone off the deep end.

I ran to the chaplain.

"Chaplain! Guess what happened to me last night!" I yelled as I burst in his door.

"From the looks of you," he laughed, "I'd say you made parole."

"Better than that! I got filled with the Holy Ghost!"

"Now, Jack, get hold of yourself," he said solemnly.

I tried to write to Carolyn. I started the letter five times, but I finally gave up.

A few days later, Mr. Lindsey came to the prison. And you can be sure I told him! He broke into a grin and slapped me on the back.

It wasn't long before I realized that none of the brothers

104

had had this experience of being "clothed with power from on high" and most of them didn't want it.

They did, however, begin to see the changes in me. I became more and more gentle. My rough edges had been chipped off. Everyone noticed that I didn't walk around with a clenched jaw anymore, trying to control my temper. They couldn't deny that the changes they saw in me were improvements, to say the least.

A couple of days after being filled with the Holy Spirit, a friend came up to me and asked, "Jack, what was that *glow* I saw coming out of your cell the other night?"

A glow? I knew my cell had been filled with the presence of God, but I didn't know there was a glow. I wanted to shout; instead, I told my friend about that night, the night that the Spirit of God came into one small cell in a dark prison, and filled a man with the power of Almighty God.

CHAPTER FIFTEEN

Revival

A few men here and there have been saved ever since I had been at Terre Haute; now they were getting saved almost every day. The Brotherhood had gradually grown to 30 members; now in a short period of time, it grew to 300 members. At last, our prayers were answered. We found ourselves in a revival. Not the kind of revival that men organized, but the kind that the Lord sends.

At first, we were amazed when a miracle took place. Then miracles began happening one right after another. The meetings of our prayer group were powerful and the Lord moved during the services to heal and save.

As word got around that a group of Terre Haute Christians were experiencing miracles, prayer requests came pouring in. We prayed for each need, and soon we'd get letters back telling us that God had answered our prayers. A loved one was saved; a relative was healed; a family was re-united.

The guards read our mail, as usual, but now the letters contained exciting reports of miracles. And some of the guards were saved.

Many of the prayer requests came from good church-goers who had been Christians all their lives. And here they were, asking for prayer from a group of former murderers, heroin addicts, rapists, bank robbers and syndicate enforcers! As Brother Lindsey had once reminded me, truly God is no respecter of persons.

A lieutenant had once asked us for prayer for his son, who had been in a bicycle accident. The boy had suffered a serious internal injury and was not expected to live through the night. We prayed and God healed the little boy. The lieutenant was convinced of the power of prayer and of the good the Brotherhood was doing. So when we lost the chapel, he was glad to let us use the Activities Room.

A few weeks later, the lieutenant changed positions and we lost the Activities Room. But one of the guards had been saved in one of our meetings, so he gave us the A. & O. Cell.

Then that guard was transferred, leaving us once again without a meeting place. But then it was summer, so we could meet outside. One of the prison yards had concrete bleachers that were perfect for meetings, so we gathered on the bleachers and went ahead praising the Lord with song and even shouts.

It wasn't long before we received a memorandum saying that prisoners couldn't meet in groups larger than ten. That presented us with a real problem. It looked like the administration had finally succeeded in disbanding the Brotherhood. But then we got an idea.

Within the prison complex was a quarter mile track that some of us had built so inmates could get some exercise. We began to meet at the track, walking up and down in groups of ten about eight feet apart. We must have been a funny sight, with all those groups of men walking up and down the track praising God with loud voices!

It wasn't long before the officials gave up and invited us back inside. They saw that we were determined to meet and that somehow we always did, and without breaking any of their rules. They gave us the education department room permanently. The Lord continued to multiply us and the revival went on and on.

I gave my testimony several times in the Brotherhood meetings, and men's lives were touched. During the revival, I was elected prison chaplain of the Wabash Valley Jaycees, and elected to positions in the Brotherhood, and these offices gave me more and more opportunities to share my story. I was always surprised when the Lord saved men through my story, although it happened over and over again.

One day in the chow hall, one of the brothers was talking to another man. The brother invited the man to a Brotherhood meeting that night to hear Happy Jack give his testimony.

"Happy Jack!" the guy exclaimed, "Are you kidding?" It turned out that the man was the same one I almost ran into the concrete pillar months earlier, and he couldn't believe that I'd be giving a *testimony*. But he was just curious enough to come to the meeting to hear for himself. At the altar call, he came forward and accepted Jesus.

Another time, a black inmate came to us for prayer, and to find out if God could possibly help him. He had been on heroin for 18 years and his veins were burned out. He couldn't live much longer in that condition. A brother and I shared with him, and he decided he wanted to accept Jesus. We took him to the chapel, and I laid hands on him and began to pray. All of a sudden, he fell to the floor. My friend and I stood there looking at each other and then at the man laid out on the floor in front of us. I was scared to death.

"Maybe he had a heart attack," I suggested. Wouldn't it be a fine thing, I thought to myself, if here he finally comes to the Lord but it's just too much for him . . .

We stood there looking down at him, not knowing what to do. In a minute, a guard walked over and looked down at him.

"Is he okay?" the guard asked, staring at him. "Maybe I should call an ambulance; he might be hurt."

"I don't think he's hurt" I answered, "because he's smiling." The man had a big grin on his face and tears were trickling down his cheeks. "Maybe he's just fainted."

A few minutes later, the man came to. It turned out that the Lord had just sort of pushed him over and saved him while he was down. He had also been healed of his heroin addiction. I found out later that this was called "being slain in the Spirit," when the power of God comes over a person in a mighty way. At the time I didn't know what in the world had happened.

The man was transferred to another prison and checked into a hospital. The officials wanted to find out what had happened to his habit and his veins. His veins were completely restored. Praise the Lord!

At 12:00 sharp, one of the inmates was supposed to throw his sugar shaker across the chow hall; that was the "official" signal for a riot to begin. When the brothers got word of the plan, we began to pray. 10:00 came, then 11:00. We kept praying. At noon, nothing happened. Soon, lunch was over and men drifted out of the chow hall. The man hadn't thrown the sugar shaker and nobody could figure out why. We never did have our summer riot. It was one of the many times the brothers prayed down riots.

One day I walked out to the prison yard for some fresh air and heard the haunting sounds of a trumpet. I looked around and saw Jim, a black inmate, sitting on one of the benches, lost in the sound of his music.

The music was so beautiful it sounded like it was from a distant angelic choir. I sat down on a bench nearby to listen. But you didn't come near Jim without his permission.

"Mind if I listen awhile?" I asked.

"So long's you don't talk," he grumbled.

Jim was serving a double life sentence. A man serving that kind of sentence will do anything. If he kills a man, what can the law do about it? Give him another life sentence? For a man without hope of ever being outside the walls of Terre Haute, the gas chamber is a blessing. Jim was the kind of prisoner the administration considered "untouchable."

He had been in for 13 years so far. He didn't belong to any of the prison groups, because he didn't want to bother with anybody's problems. He was a loner, drifting through the halls like a shadow, rarely speaking to anyone or associating with anyone. The only escape he had from his private hell was his trumpet.

I pulled out my New Testament and began reading. In a minute, he put his trumpet down and stared at me.

"You don't believe that thing you're reading, do you?" he sneered. "I sure don't believe any man walked on water, healed the lame and raised the dead . . . you don't believe it, do you?

"I sure do," I answered, "and can I tell you why?"

"Yeah," he said slowly, "Go ahead."

I told him my testimony, what I had been before, how the Lord trapped me in the back seat of a police car, about that day in Albuquerque. I told him that Jesus had made me a new person, a loving person, and only He could do that.

He listened to every word. When I finished, he asked if he could play a couple of songs for me. He played "Onward Christian Soldiers," and "The Church in the Wildwood." I won't hear more beautiful music until I hear Gabriel play his trumpet in Heaven.

Before I left, Jim said he'd like to talk to me again some time. The next weekend my family was coming, so I didn't go to the yard. But the following Saturday, I met Jim again. When he asked where I had been last Saturday, I saw that he was serious about wanting to talk some more.

Every weekend after that, we'd meet in the yard. I'd talk about the Lord, and he'd pretend not to hear. But I knew he was interested. If there was a power that could help him endure the rest of his life, what did he have to lose? Finally, after two months of meeting in the yard, he asked if he could sit with the brothers at meals. I realized God was gradually breaking through that shell Jim had built around himself. If a man wanted to hear conversation about Jesus three times a day, well, who could deny him! Blacks and whites didn't sit together in the chow hall; there was no rule against it—they just didn't do it. But I knew the brothers wouldn't mind having Jim eat with us, and I sure didn't. I told Jim we'd be glad to have him. As far as I knew, it was the first time in 13 years that Jim had wanted to associate with *anyone*.

At the next meal, Jim was there. From then on, he was there at every meal. He never said much; he just listened.

A few weeks later, I heard that a black preacher, Rev. Ray Russell, was coming to preach at the prison. He had come once before, and I liked him. He was a powerful speaker. If I could get Jim to go hear him, he just might be saved. But that wasn't going to be easy.

"There's a preacher coming next week," I told Jim at the next meal, "and you'd like him. Want to come to the meeting to hear him?"

"No way!" he snapped back, "I don't want no part of no cliques." He didn't want to go *that* far in the Brotherhood. I still felt that he had to go to that meeting. The day arrived, but he still refused to even consider it.

When I was called on to say grace at supper, only a few

hours before the meeting, I prayed, "Lord, You know how much we want Jim to come to the meeting tonight. I'm asking you, Lord, to touch his heart and give him a desire to come tonight." It was a last-ditch effort, and I thought I had failed. Jim sat beside me with his head bowed while I finished praying, and during the meal he acted like he hadn't even heard me.

The time came for the service to begin. I looked around the chapel, but there was no sign of Jim. Rev. Russell was introduced; still no Jim. As he began his sermon, however, I saw the chapel door open a few inches and I turned around. Jim was standing outside the door, listening—at a safe distance. Throughout the sermon, I prayed with all my heart that the Lord would touch Jim.

"I was a Baptist preacher's son," Rev. Russell said as he came to the close of his sermon, "but I was as lost as any bank robber, murderer, or rapist, because I didn't have a personal relationship with the Son of God." I was praying so hard my heart was pounding 90 miles an hour. Suddenly, the door opened and Jim slipped onto a seat on the back row.

"If there is any man here tonight," Rev. Russell continued, "who wants that peace and joy in their heart that only Jesus Christ of Nazareth can give, I'm asking you to come to this altar . . ."

I heard the sound of feet *running*, and saw Jim flying down the aisle with tears streaming down his face. He couldn't wait to get to that altar. He hit the floor a few feet from the altar and slid the rest of the way on his knees. A hundred hands were laid on him as we gathered around, praying and praising God. When Jim stood up a few minutes later, and wiped his tears, he had a grin all over his face. He looked like a different person.

He had a grin on his face all the time after that; and he was a man who *never* smiled before. We used to kid him about his "piano keys." That big smile was contagious.

One day, another black, who was a minister in a militant black religion, stopped Jim in the hall.

"What's happened to you, man?" he asked, "I've been locked up with you for nine years, and I've never seen you so happy. I've never seen you happy at all."

Jim told him exactly why he was so happy. Jesus had made him a new person; Jesus was the reality he had searched for all his life; Jesus had given him a new heart.

My god can't do that for me!" the militant exclaimed, "I want your Jesus." Jim led him in prayer, and before that man walked on down the hall, he was a new member of the family of God.

Joe's conversion changed my attitude toward militants, especially those in a false religion. I never had liked those militants, and frankly, I really disliked Joe. But I saw that God could save a militant just as easily as He could a bank robber; Jesus loved militants, even those who worshipped another god, so I had to love them too.

Not long after Joe became a Christian, some followers of his former religion attacked him in the hall. Their minister was a traitor; he had gone over to the enemy, the "blue-eyed blonde-haired devils" and the white man's god. They cut Joe across the abdomen with a shank and left him in the hall to die. The guards rushed him to the hospital, but the doctors said he probably wouldn't live until morning.

The doctors worked on Joe for 6½ hours, trying to sew him back up. He had been slashed nine times, and his intestines were in shreds. The doctors got them back together, but he had lost too much blood.

As soon as the brothers heard the news, we began a 24-hour prayer vigil. Joe had a tremendous witness in the prison because of his old religion. The Lord had given him to us, and we weren't going to let a false god take him away.

It was my special prayer that God would spare Joe so I could repent of my prejudice and lack of love toward him. Here was a man who just weeks before had been screaming angrily about the white god and the oppression of the blacks. But after his conversion, he had been willing to *die* for Jesus, the "white god." When he accepted Jesus, he knew the dangers, but he was willing to risk it all.

When I went to work the next morning, one of the officials commented to me, "Well, another one's bit the dust."

"What do you mean?" I asked.

"The black—he's dead."

"No he's not!" I exclaimed, "He can't be. He's alive."

The official remembered Joe's conversion to Christianity, and realized how I felt about him. He looked at me sympathetically and said, "I'm sorry . . . But he's dead."

My heart sank to my shoes, but somehow I couldn't accept the fact that Joe had died. He *couldn't* be dead.

When the official got back from lunch, he told me the news. "You were right . . . the black's not dead. In fact, *he's holding his own at the hospital.*" He shook his head in disbelief.

The recovery was long and painful. As soon as Joe could have visitors, I went to see him. I told him that I loved him and accepted him as a brother in Jesus. Tears welled in his eyes—and mine. He had so much company from the Brotherhood that I think we must have *loved* him into complete recovery.

Six weeks later, Joe could move around in a wheelchair. The men who tried to kill him never tried it again. *They* were terrified of *him*. They knew what they had done to him was fatal, so they looked upon him as a man raised from the dead. By the power of God, he was. They stayed as far away from him as possible.

But still, because of Joe's conversion, numbers of militants turned to Jesus over the years. The message of the gospel spread on and on throughout Terre Haute, saving, healing and unifying.

Jim, the beautiful black brother with the big smile was paroled a few years later. And parole from a double life sentence doesn't happen every day. I learned that soon after Jim was out, he was killed in a construction accident on the job. I don't know why God took him home just as he was starting a new life. I don't understand it, but God does.

I do know one thing. One day we will be in fellowship again in our Father's house. We will sit down and eat together at the same table again. Perhaps he and Gabriel are playing duets on their trumpets right now.

The revival really never ended. Some of the brothers were transferred to other prisons, and wherever they went, they set up prayer meetings and began to pray for the power of God to fall. The story of our Terre Haute revival repeated itself over and over again across the nation, and the results of our fast are still being felt today.

I have met inmates who have never seen me before, but they know me because of the revival. Often I'll have a prisoner come up to me and say, "You're the Happy Jack who was at Terre Haute when that big revival started. You led Frank to the Lord and Frank led Sam to the Lord, and Sam led *me* to the Lord."

CHAPTER SIXTEEN

The 'Thirty-One Day' Miracle

When the parole board came to Terre Haute, about every 18 months, I was always one of the first in line outside the office where the parole officer would be working and reviewing cases.

Guards laughed when they saw me. "Give up, Burbridge," they'd advise. "You'll never make it. You'll be here until September, 1975." Even the parole officer just shook his head and sent me away when he saw me at the door.

September of 1975 was the earliest parole date I could get with the good time I had accumulated in almost 3½ years. That was the *earliest*. It was now 1970. If I made one wrong move, all my good time would be erased, and my parole date would go back to the full 12 years of my sentence; in that case, I'd get out in October, 1979.

In spite of all the advice I was getting, I still went before the parole officer every chance I got. It hurt a little when I was turned down; it would be a long time before he came back. But I was determined not to get discouraged. I wasn't going to give up. I wanted to be available just in case the Lord wanted to get me out. When Jesus shook the prison doors open and set the captives free like He did in the Bible, I didn't want to be way off on the other side of the prison; I was going to stick beside that door!

In October of 1970, the parole officer came back to the prison. I dutifully went to see him. When I appeared at the door, he motioned to me.

"Come in, Burbridge," he said, "and sit down."

I had never gotten that far before. He had never invited me in. My heart started pounding. The officer put a disc on his recording machine. He would record our conversation and play the disc back at a meeting of the full parole board.

"Burbridge," he began, patting my thick FBI file, "I've been looking over your record. You've been pretty bad. You have here a record of violence. Yet, you've been here in Terre Haute for over three years, and you don't have one red mark against your name. How do you account for that?"

He started the recorder and I started talking. I told him my whole testimony, beginning with that day in Albuquerque. The disc ran out, and he flipped it over to the other side. That side almost ran out before I finished my story.

"Do you mean," he said thoughtfully, "that you don't give any credit to this institution for your rehabilitation and this change in your life?"

"Sir, let me tell you something," I answered after a moment's hesitation, "If anything, this institution is a detriment to helping a man fit back into society and straighten out his life. I don't see how any man makes it here without the Lord .. ."

"We'll contact you in a few weeks," he interrupted. He closed my file quickly and slid it aside.

I thought about the officer all that week. I may have blown my chances when I told him that the institution had not helped me. I knew what he wanted to hear; he wanted me to praise Terre Haute. I had to be honest; Jesus and

117

Jesus *alone* had been responsible for my "rehabilitation." I tried to analyze the officer; I wrote a long letter to Carolyn about him. He could have been a Christian, testing me to see if I was for real; he could have been an atheist who just didn't believe me.

The worst that could happen would be that I wouldn't make parole. If I kept my good time, which I knew I could, I would be in Terre Haute only another five years. That seemed like such a long time, but I didn't forget that I could have been in prison for 45 years. If it weren't for the mercy of God, I could have been in Terre Haute until the year 2012!

Parole was a slow, tedious process, and even when parole was granted, it was usually between three to 18 months before it went into effect. So if I did get parole, I would still be in prison probably another year. I settled back and tried not to think about it. But that was hard.

Two months passed without any word from the parole board. I would cringe inside when I thought of the parole board members looking over my FBI file and shaking their heads. To the non-Christian it seems impossible that a man could change instantly, after a lifetime in crime. A man *can't* change instantly; he has to start over; he has to be born again. What happened to me wasn't "self-betterment," or "turning over a new leaf." It was rebirth. But the non-Christian can't understand that.

One day, on December 7, 1970, a guard gave me the message that the parole officer wanted to see me. I went to the office; sat down, and tried to prepare myself for the news. From the look on the officer's face, I was about to be either rejected or put off for another 18 months.

But then he broke into a smile.

"Burbridge, are you ready to go home?" he asked calmly.

"Sir, I was ready to go home before I got here!" I

exclaimed excitedly, "After three years in a 6' x 10' cell, yes, Sir, I'm ready to go home."

"How about January?" He was grinning now.

I figured fast. Thirteen months until next January. Exactly one year and one month! I held my breath.

"Can I call my wife and children and tell them they can pick me up in 13 months for sure?" I asked.

"You can call them tonight," he answered, "but they can't pick you up in 13 months."

My heart sank to my shoes. It would be the following January, 25 months. But that was better than five years. The officer didn't speak for a moment, as he watched my face.

"You can tell them to come get you in 31 days," he finally said.

January; a *month* away. It was December 7 now; I could leave on January 8—*31 days*. I was stunned. I couldn't believe it.

"Sir, thank you, Sir," I said in a daze, "Praise the Lord! Thank you, Sir!" He laughed and congratulated me.

The brothers told me not to get my hopes up. The prison officials told me not to get my hopes up. They were sure there had been a mistake. Nobody got parole in one month. Every day, I expected to be called into the warden's office to hear the words, "Sorry, Burbridge, but there's been a slight adjustment in your parole date . . ."

The days passed. Nothing happened. I was going to be a free man. I was excited, grateful . . . and a little apprehensive. What would happen now? I had no career—crime had been my career before. I thought about all my old friends, how they were expecting me to go back to work with them. It seemed like an eternity since I had been *that* Happy Jack. But how would my old buddies react to this new one?

They were all expecting to see me again, except J.K. A

119

few months earlier, I had heard the news. J.K. had been killed in a fight over an 18-year old prostitute. He had come along and swept the young girl off her feet—and away from a kid who loved her. One day as J.K. and the girl were driving along a highway, the kid followed them and drove them off the road. J.K. jumped out of the car, mad as a hornet, and headed for the kid. When he saw how mad J. K. was, he pulled out his gun and shot him. A few hours later, J.K. died at the hospital. It struck me as ironic that he was dead—because of a young prostitute—and *I* was alive, healed, delivered and about to leave prison to begin a new life, the "good life."

What a difference between us! That was the difference *Jesus* made. I had often wondered why the Lord had done so much for me, and yet left others, like J.K., to go on their way to destruction. Unless the Lord saved J.K. in a split second before his death, he had died without Jesus. I know one reason God saved me—because of my praying family. I had someone pounding on the door of heaven for me night and day. I had someone bombarding the throne of grace on my behalf every night with the cry, "Lord, *save* my son!" I had my Mom, the prayer warrior, who wouldn't leave God alone until He had granted her request.

The morning of January 8 finally arrived. I was almost afraid to breathe. If I got a red mark, I'd lose my parole, even now.

I packed my books and Bible studies. A guard came by to tell me that I had to wait for the morning mail delivery at 9:30. The Officials were still convinced there had been a mistake, and they were sure a letter would come in the morning mail, informing them of the mistake. But the mail came, and there was no notice. It was time to go.

I went to my cell and gathered up my belongings. There had been a stream of visitors that morning, brothers coming by to tell me good-bye. I would miss them very much. They had been my friends and partners for over three years. I told them I'd come see them. I knew how much it meant to have visitors. I'd never forget our years together, suffering together, rejoicing together as we saw hundreds of men come to know the Lord.

My cell was empty. My prison uniform lay on the cot. I stood at the door and glanced at the cell once more. That drab concrete room was the place I had gotten to know Jesus. I had spent hours on my knees there. I had learned His Word there. He had met me every night in that 6' x 10' cell.

A brother came by to help me with the two large boxes that contained everything I owned. Each of us lifted a box and we walked across the range and down to the front desk. We shook hands and he left. A guard would escort me out to the parking lot across the street, where my family was waiting for me at that moment.

The guard glanced at my two boxes and announced, "If you want them outta here, you got to carry them." But there was nothing that the devil could throw at me that morning to get my eyes off Jesus.

I felt like I was breaking in two when I picked up both boxes. I just had to pray for strength. When we got to the front door, the guard opened the door, rushed through, and let it close behind him. Fortunately, the door opened outward, so I just pushed through. The bitter cold air hit my face; every muscle in my arms and back were on fire; I could hardly breathe; but I could see Carolyn's car across the street. That's all I needed.

A guard in the main tower had been informed that we were coming, so he pushed a button to open the huge main gate when he spotted us. I heard a loud buzz as the big steel gates slowly opened. The guard slipped through the gate, and pulled it in behind him so I couldn't get through. But I lunged forward with all the strength I could muster, and I was able to stick my foot in the gate, pull it open, and hurry through it. *Just a little longer, Lord,* I silently prayed, *"just a little longer. . ."*

We crossed the street to the parking lot. When Carolyn saw me, she jumped out and opened the tailgate of our station wagon for me to put the boxes down. She saw from my face I was about to collapse. Just as I started to lower the boxes, the guard stopped me. He was determined.

"Just a minute before you set them down," he ordered. "Mrs. Burbridge, I need to see your identification." This guard had seen Carolyn visiting me for years, and he knew her as well as he did me.

Poor Carolyn! She had been told to pick me up at 8:30 that morning. But she was so excited, she arrived almost a half an hour earlier. Then the morning mail delayed me. Now, it was almost 10:00. The car had over-heated when she let it idle, so she and the children had been waiting almost two hours in below-freezing weather.

Carolyn was so cold that she couldn't find her I.D. card in her purse. She kept fumbling because her hands were so cold. When she took off her gloves, I saw that her fingers were red and stiff. She finally handed her I.D. card to the guard and he examined it for five minutes. When he had read every word on the front and the back, he handed it slowly back to Carolyn.

"Okay," he mumbled, and unable to do anything else, he turned and started back for the prison. I dropped the boxes on the tailgate with a groan of relief and jumped into the car. And I was at last a free man. To me, the vast gray sky and barren landscape looked like spring.

It felt wonderful—and strange—to be with my family and hold them without a dozen pairs of eyes on us. Jackie and Vern couldn't stop hugging me and crying, "Daddy! Daddy!" I knew we were, in so many ways, strangers, but that didn't matter to them. It was as though the sound of that beautiful word, "daddy," made up for all else! And besides, I *would* make everything up to them. We wouldn't be strangers for long. At times, they would look up into my face with their big round eyes, and I saw such trust on their faces. I was grateful.

Carolyn drove to the motel in town. She had to drive, because I didn't have a license. But if I had, I probably would have wrecked us—when she pulled out of the parking lot going 30 mph, it felt like we were doing 110 mph. As we turned toward town, I took one last look at Terre Haute.

At the motel room, my family had a surprise for me. When I walked in the door, our little poodle, Lover, almost turned wrong side out with joy. I sat down and he jumped in my lap, put his paws around my neck and just cried. I almost cried too.

That morning, we had breakfast with Jimmy Kline, the Gideon who had given me my first Gideon Bible when I arrived at Terre Haute. I showed it to Jimmy. The pages were worn and, he knew, well read.

As we started the long drive back to South Bend, I thought about all the Christians who had come to visit us, to support and encourage us. I never forgot what their love and kindness meant to us.

"I was in prison and you visited me . . ." Jesus said. It separated the sheep from the goats.

I was 33 years old; I had a whole lifetime in front of me. "Lord," I prayed as I watched the countryside flying by outside the window, "My life is Yours. Lord, You open the doors and I'll go through them."

CHAPTER SEVENTEEN

A Nice, Quiet Job

I leaned comfortably against the back of the armchair and watched Carolyn as she finished the last of the Sunday dinner dishes. I had eaten too much. But then I couldn't get enough of her cooking.

We had stayed up all night Friday, talking about our plans for the future. I would relax for a month, then find a job as a payroll accountant/time study keeper in one of the large factories in the area. If I couldn't get a factory job, I had some other ideas. At any rate, I would find a nice, quiet 8:00 to 5:00 job and, on the side, go through whatever doors the Lord opened for me.

Carolyn's church had given me a Homecoming dinner Saturday night. The church members had loved and encouraged Carolyn while I was in Terre Haute, and now they welcomed me home like an old friend. There was even some talk of my working with the church, possibly as a youth director. But I would consider church-related work only as a last resort; I wanted that nice, quiet 8:00 to 5:00 job.

Tonight, Carolyn and I were going to Calvary Temple, a large church in South Bend. The lively worship wouldn't be new to her, however. When Rocky, a brother from

Terre Haute, was paroled a few months earlier, I had asked him to take Carolyn and the kids to Calvary Temple. She agreed to go with him to Calvary Temple, if he would go to her church. She and the kids went to Calvary Temple once with Rocky, but over the next several months she went back, taking others with her. She thought the Pentecostals were crazy, but she admired their "spirit."

A knock at the door interrupted my thoughts. A man introduced himself as John Smith, president of the local Gideon chapter and a friend of Jimmy Kline's. Would I consider, John asked, speaking at the chapter meeting tomorrow night? The scheduled speaker was a doctor, who wanted to give up his slot on the program to hear my story. I glanced at Carolyn; she just smiled.

At the meeting, I gave a brief testimony. At the invitation of Emmet and Susanna Eiler, whom we met after the meeting, Carolyn and I went to our first Full Gospel Business Men's Fellowship International meeting that same week. Over the years, Carolyn and I would have a long and fruitful association with both the Gideons and FGBMFI.

Within a couple of weeks, I began receiving other invitations to speak—at churches, fellowships and even civic clubs. At one civic club meeting, I ended up sitting beside the only cigar smoker in the crowd and I almost got sick from the smoke. Only God can take a man who managed a cigar store and smoked stogies all day and turn him into a man who can't even stand the smell of the smoke!

The first few times Carolyn heard my testimony, she just shook her head in amazement. Only then did she learn about Philadelphia, the bomb in my car, the enforcement, the prostitution and everything else. Later, when I first heard *her* testimony, I cried like a baby. Only then did *I* learn what I had put her through.

When I was in Terre Haute, I had a growing burden for young people. I hated to see kids come to Terre Haute; they'd try to act tough and talk tough, about the cops, the judges, their old ladies. But I discovered I had a rapport with them. For one thing, I could "out-tough" them. Anything they had done, I had done it better. Once I got their attention, I could talk about the Lord and they'd listen. A lot of them were saved, but it always bothered me that they were in prison in the first place. As I prayed about these kids, the Lord gave me an idea.

Two weeks after I got home, I took the idea to Gene "Nifty" Norris, an FBI agent who had once worked on my case. He had heard about my conversion, and believed it. As I told him my plan, he listened with interest. I wanted to team up with a policeman who had known me before, and go into the area high schools. We could reach the kids *before* they even got started in crime—and the combination of a "cop and robber" would get their attention!

"Well, Jack," Gene said approvingly, "Got anybody in mind . . . like Ralph Wolfe?"

Ralph, my old buddy. I had thought of him. Our "relationship" went all the way back to my early days in the service, to the night we fought in the snow. Ralph had seen it all; he had watched me go from a hot-headed kid to enforcer to bank robber to heroin addict. There was only one problem. He never believed for one minute that I had really become a Christian.

Gene offered to call Ralph to get his reaction. In a few minutes, Gene came back to his desk with the bad news.

"He says nothing doing," Gene reported. "He says the only way he wants to see you is in a casket." But I was still convinced that Ralph was the right man for the team.

That night, Ralph told his wife, Nancy, about "that crazy Happy Jack." But Nancy's reaction was different.

"Ralph," she commented, "If the Lord can forgive Jack, then you should be able to." When Ralph went to bed, he couldn't sleep. He tossed and turned for hours, struggling with the idea of actually *forgiving* me.

That night, Carolyn and I went to a prayer meeting. We all prayed together that Ralph would change his mind, or at least consent to see me. The meeting ended at about 12:30. At 3:00 that morning, Ralph, still unable to sleep woke Nancy and told her he had "given up." He would talk to me, and, he guessed, go along with the plan.

At breakfast that morning, Ralph's daughter commented, "That's neat, Dad—a cop and a con . . ." It did have a nice ring.

When I answered my telephone, I heard that old familiar voice. It hadn't changed a bit. "You wanted to see me?" Ralph grumbled.

"Yes, I would," I answered. "Could you come out to my house this afternoon?"

"No *way*," he snapped, "If you want to see me, you come to Room 210 in the Police Department." And he slammed down the receiver.

Ralph sat with his head bent over a stack of papers on his desk when I walked in. He was scribbling furiously.

"Good morning, *Sir*," I said politely.

"Sit down," he ordered.

"Yes, *Sir*."

His head popped up.

Over the next few days, Ralph and I designed a program for kids and we began receiving invitations to speak. He had only two conditions he wanted met before he joined me on the program—that the name of the presentation be "The Cop and the Con," and that he be allowed to say anything he wanted to. I was glad to agree to both.

We couldn't preach in the schools, but we could tell about our feud, my conversion, and the "rewards of

127

crime." We began each program by asking the kids to guess which one of us was the cop. The Lord had done so much with my appearance that they usually chose *me*. Ralph would laugh and start telling the kids about this "cop" he had with him. We could see mouths falling open all over the auditorium.

When Ralph finished, I told of all the loneliness and pain, briefly about the drive to Albuquerque with Mr. Lytton, and about my conversion. I couldn't give an altar call, but that didn't stop the Lord. In every school, lives were touched and changed as the kids opened their hearts. The program was welcomed in schools because it was an effective deterrent against crime; kids who were headed toward crime at least thought twice about it. The area was a high crime district and the Cop and the Con program got a lot of attention.

After each program, we invited the kids to a local church where we would be speaking that night, in case they wanted to hear more about the *new* life. They came by droves. Tough kids; nice kids; Sunday school kids; kids on dope; they all came.

And of course, the most impressive part of the program was the story of the vendetta between Ralph and me, two men on opposite sides of the law now reconciled in Christ.

Shortly after I began speaking publicly, I ran into an unusual problem—my language. At a sunrise service in Plymouth, Indiana, in the first large church I had spoken in, I noticed puzzled expressions in the crowd, but I didn't know why. I gradually realized that the congregation didn't understand half what I was saying. Afterwards, when the pastor, Darrell Kraft, and I talked, I shared the problem with him. He didn't help much. "Well, Jack, I have to admit," he said sheepishly, "I'd like to know what 'woofing a reefer' means." I saw that I'd have to re-learn English; all I had spoken for 34 years was street English.

Slowly, I was able to translate my street English by speaking into a tape recorder and listening to myself—for hours. It was like learning a foreign language.

I soon realized that I might be telling my story often, perhaps the rest of my life. People responded to my story and it seemed my testimony traveled faster than I could. For every one engagement I was able to meet, it seemed that 10 more sprung up to take its place.

Each time I spoke, I had to re-live certain scenes from the past, and it was like digging up an old corpse. I wanted to share my story, but just not so often and certainly not as a *career*. Giving my testimony seemed to keep me living in the past and as a result the old guilt would crawl up the back of my neck and whisper in my ear, "Jack, old buddy, that man was *you—you* did those things." One morning after a church service where I had spoken, I was so overcome I had to walk around outside the church to get some fresh air. The scenes I had just described in my testimony were as vivid as they were in the nightmares I had once had, and I felt sick to my stomach.

As I paced outside the church, the Lord spoke to me clearly, saying, "Look, son, that man you talk about doesn't exist any more. He died, and you are *not* that man." The reality of being *born* again suddenly struck me. When I was born again, I was like a brand new baby coming into the world; and the old man died in "childbirth!" The scripture I had quoted so often, "If any man be in Christ, he is a new creature," took on new and deeper meaning for me and from that day on I never had a problem with the old man—no matter how often he tried to rise up out of his grave.

In August of my first year home, Carolyn was filled with the Holy Spirit. Since I had gotten home in January, she had gone with me to FGBMFI meetings, prayer meetings and churches. She was ready for the Holy Spirit that day as she sat in a Katherine Kuhlman meeting at Notre Dame and felt a sudden love surge over her again and again. She had never felt such peace. A couple of days later, she realized she had been filled with the Holy Spirit. A month later, both my children were filled with the Spirit.

Now, we were united, not only physically but spiritually. For the first time in 10 years of fatherhood, I reviewed report cards, bandaged scraped knees, wiped away tears, prayed with my children and taught them the Scriptures. In the process, I fulfilled the vision I had on the road to Albuquerque—to be the kind of family man Mr. Lytton was.

The Cop and the Con program, conducted in my old stomping grounds, created some disturbance. Officially, I was clean with the syndicate, because I hadn't informed on anyone, even though I could have put a lot of people away. But some individuals still thought I was a traitor, riding around with a cop and telling kids how rotten the criminal life is.

One day, I ran into J.B., an old friend, and I shared with him. When I finished, he looked me square in the eyes and said, "You know, don't you, Hap, that I'm going to have to kill you the next time I see you?" No, I didn't know, but I said something amiable and we parted.

A few weeks later, I walked into a restaurant and spotted J.B. in a booth. I went to his table and sat down across from him, with my back to the door. He shifted to expose the gun in his belt.

"Remember what you told me that last time I saw you?" I asked.

"Yeah," he said slowly, "I remember."

"Well, you'd better be careful," I continued. He naturally took it as a threat; but at least this was the old Happy Jack he had known! He looked me over and saw I wasn't even armed.

"What do you mean?" he asked suspiciously.

"If you pull that trigger," I answered, "It might just backfire and blow your brains out. My Bible says that Jesus holds the keys to life and death, and my schedule is too full for me to die now . . ."

Cursing loudly, J.B. jumped up from the table, knocking over his coke and water glasses, and stormed out of the restaurant. He was furious. The manager even came over to find out what I said to make him so mad. I told him.

I discovered that even the toughest sinner has a terrible fear of God and His Word. J.B. couldn't handle the possibility that his gun *might* backfire, since Jesus *might* hold the keys to life and death, since that was in the Bible, which just *might* be the Word of God. It's not that bad characters hate God; they're just scared to death of Him.

One night Ralph and I spoke in a church in Gary, one of my main territories when I was in the syndicate. J.K. and I had worked it together during the power struggle, and a lot of men knew me well. After the service, two men who had known me came up to Ralph.

"Man, you pulled a bummer," one sneered.

"What do you mean?" Ralph asked.

"That ain't Happy Jack," the man announced. "It looks sort of like him, but it ain't him. Whatja do with the old man? Kill him?"

Ralph called me over to the two men. When they saw that I really was Happy Jack, one of them wheeled around and left the church. The other one just shook his head and muttered, "It's a good sham, Hap; it *sure* is a good sham." He kept shaking his head in disbelief. He couldn't get over the changes in me.

To many of my old friends, trying to talk to me was like talking to a stranger who was occupying Happy Jack's old body. When I showed the old pictures of me from the newspapers in churches or schools, people couldn't be-

131

lieve I was the same person, *physically*. The main difference was the look in my eyes. Jesus said that the eyes are the light of the body, and so if the eyes are dark, the whole body is dark. That's what I looked like in the old pictures; I was a *being* of darkness walking around in human form. That's why the man in the church service in Gary told Ralph that I looked "sort of *like* Happy Jack" but wasn't him. I wasn't dark any more.

The rumor finally went around in syndicate circles that I was keeping up the sham until I got off parole, then I would come back to work. But on my wedding anniversay, June 24, 1975, the letter came; I was off parole.

Three months after I got home, Kate, J.K.'s old ace, came by the house to see me. J.K.'s death had shaken her, and she had dropped out of the business. Now she was living with a pusher. When she asked if I was going back into the business, I told her the whole story of my conversion in Albuquerque and all that Jesus had done in my life. When I told her about the heroin miracle, she put her face in her hands and cried. She had come off heroin cold turkey, and alone.

Ralph and I saw hundreds of kids come to Jesus through the Cop and the Con program. Over a year's time, we crisscrossed the state, often visiting high schools all over the west and mid-west. After a year, a political re-shuffle took place in the police department and Ralph could no longer participate in the program. But the Lord opened other doors for me and soon I was traveling almost constantly. When FGBMFI's *Voice* magazine carried my testimony, the number of invitations soared. And all the miracles we witnessed during the years of our ministry would fill another book.

And somehow, I never got around to find that nice, quiet 8:00 to 5:00 job in a factory.

CHAPTER EIGHTEEN

Back Inside

Since 1971, I've logged between 75,000 and 100,000 miles a year.

I've traveled all over the United States, Canada, Mexico and Europe.

But I've also been back to prison, hundreds of times. I go to prison every chance I get, in fact! Two weeks after I got out of Terre Haute, I visited the local county jail and I've been in jails ever since, ministering, preaching, teaching and counseling, telling prisoners what Jesus can do with a life that's hit rock-bottom.

I've seen hard-core killers racked with sobs when they discover that Jesus died for them. I've seen inmates delivered of drugs and every other bondage under the sun. I've given my story in untold hundreds—maybe thousands—of churches, conventions, meetings and clubs, but prisons are still closest to my heart. I'd go to a prison any where, any time, any way I could get there.

I beleive that's the main reason God called me to the ministry—to send me back to the prisons, to the men who live like I did. That's God's "evangelism program"— fishermen telling fishermen the good news; tax collectors telling other tax collectors; neighbors telling neighbors; Gentiles telling Gentiles; thieves telling other thieves.

When I was in Terre Haute, a lot of well-meaning preachers often began their sermons by announcing, "I was in prison once." The men perked up, all set to hear how he went from prison to preaching. Then the preacher sighed, "Yes, I was in a prison of *sin*." My heart always sank to my shoes. The inmates wanted to punch him in the nose; to them, it was deceit, just a trick to get their attention. It made them so mad they just tuned him out and didn't accept anything else he had to say. I know the preacher thought he was doing a good thing by identifying with the men; but he didn't understand that there's nothing quite like a prison built of steel and concrete.

When I tell a group of inmates that I was in prison, and back it up with "I was in for 3½ years at Terre Haute, Indiana," they listen. They're not interested in my testimony, however. They don't want to know *at first* how I was saved; their question is "How did you get out?" They want to know how I made it out, physically and mentally and for keeps. In other words, they want to know how I survived.

Survival. That's the key. Men in prison are surrounded by the harsher realities of life, such as death, hunger, sleep, boredom, food poisoning. The only real question is "Will I get out? Will I make it?" They go to sleep at night staring at four gray walls; they wake up the next morning staring at the same four gray walls. An inmate spends his time trying not to wonder about the future . . . whether or not his wife or girlfriend will be waiting when he gets out, whether he will hear from the outside. . .

The answer is to find a reality that is *stronger* than those around him. And that's where Jesus comes in. An inmate will try anything to survive—drugs, sex, money *or* Jesus.

I can see now that my years at Terre Haute were

training for the ministry. Terre Haute was my seminary, and I graduated. I have a degree in prison ministries. My past life and years I spent at Terre Haute give me credibility with the men, and that's all I need. Credibility goes a long way in prison, because most inmates are like geiger counters when they sense a phony.

I never have trouble getting permission to speak in a prison; officials run a check on me, see that I am successfully "rehabilitated" and open the doors. Most prison officials are genuinely devoted to seeing men rehabilitated; anyone who can offer a hope of that will be heard. The prison systems in some states have tried color television sets and carpeted floors and these things *are* good; the only thing wrong with them is that they don't work. They make a man comfortable, but they don't make him change.

If an inmate tries to tell me he's happy, I can call him a liar, because I've been there. If he tries to tell me he's running his life okay without God, I can ask him why, if he's doing such a great job with his life, I am standing there talking to him through a wall of bars. I've been there, too—running my life, always in control of my life, but I ended up the same way—in prison. I've never had a man throw anything, any argument, at me that I couldn't say, "Man, I've been there. I tried that." But I don't go into a prison with the attitude that the men will automatically believe me.

I can appeal to a man's head and circumstances, but only the Holy Spirit can reach a man's heart. Sometimes an inmate will readily admit to being a sinner, but not to committing the sin that put him in prison in the first place. The crime which got him a sentence wasn't his fault—it's always someone else's fault; someone framed him; someone dropped the dime. When I was arrested, the simple fact that I was guilty of robbing banks never once crossed my mind. All I thought about was the set-up. I knew I was a bad character; deep down I knew I was a sinner, but I wouldn't have used that word. What I needed was to really *see* myself. That's what happened that night in Amarillo, Texas.

Only Jesus by the Holy Spirit working in the heart can reveal a man to himself. That terrible night in Amarillo was necessary for my conversion the next day. Somehow, I had always accepted my way of life as normal, because over the years my sense of right and wrong had become distorted beyond all hope. I didn't know there was anything actually wrong with my way of life until I saw myself through God's eyes. And it was literal hell.

God had to show me His standards, in the form of Mr. Lytton, before I could see how bad off I was. In the back of the police car, it was as though God put His arm around me and said, "Look, Jack, Mr. Lytton is My kind of man; he lives My kind of *life*. Look at it . . . isn't it so much better and satisfying than yours? Son, wouldn't you like to live that kind of life. . .?" My answer was, "I desperately want to live like he does."

I believe that God has a perfect moment planned to confront every person in the world with that knowledge and that choice. It's a beautiful moment, but it's also agonizing. God does it all, not the preacher.

So when I go into prisons, I see myself as another Mr. Lytton. I pray that the men will see in my life what I saw in his. If they compare my life with theirs, the conclusion is simple; we started out in the same boat, but I got my life straight and they didn't. They don't want to be preachers, no more than I want to be a cop because of what I saw in Mr. Lytton; but they do want to be free, just like I did. I just try to present my story and my life—and let the men see the difference Jesus makes.

When a man hears that Jesus is that power and reality

who can set men free from their bondages, reunite families, walk the halls of prison with them, and open the prison doors, well, what does he have to lose? Nothing. And he has everything to gain. The first time I preached a revival in a prison, I was shocked to see half the crowd come pouring down the aisle for the altar call. On the outside, a man has nothing to lose when he gives his life to Christ, but he doesn't realize it. When he may have to give up his new job, or car,or affair or booze, it's not as obvious to him that he has nothing to lose. But a man in prison *knows* he has nothing to lose.

I'm not saying that all prisoners will be saved—but I imagine that about half of them will. When Jesus was crucified, He had two thieves beside him and *half* of them were saved. The thief who was saved made the comparison between his life and Jesus'. His conclusion was that Jesus was a holy, righteous man who had done nothing to deserve death; he on the other hand, was a sinner who deserved to die because he was guilty. It was his moment of confrontation, and he was saved.

Once when I was leaving a state prison near Atmore, Alabama after preaching, a guard stopped me and offered some friendly advice. "Preacher," he said knowingly, "You're wasting your time. Those men will never change. They're just animals." I didn't have time to talk with him, but I smiled, stuck a copy of my testimony in his hand and walked on. I would love to have seen the look on his face when he found out that this preacher hadn't always been a preacher.

What this guard didn't understand is that we are all animals and criminals. We're born criminals and unless somewhere along the line God Himself comes to live in us, we die criminals. The problem is that some crimes are not illegal. There are no laws against some crimes. One criminal may rob a bank because he wants money; another criminal may ruin his family by chasing the dollar for 20 years because he wants money. Who is to say which is worse—outright stealing $25,000, or driving your wife to another man and your children to drugs, cults, crime, or even suicide (the number one killers of kids today is themselves)? The motive in both cases is greed; that greed just took different forms.

We have laws against murder, rape, stealing and the like. We have no laws against lust, greed and hate, all those motives behind the crimes. The only difference between inmates and others is that inmates have crossed the line of what is *legally* acceptable. But in God's eyes, sin is sin, and He's more interested in the source of sin, our own human natures that need to be completely transformed, than He is in what form that sin takes. That's why He can love the sinner while He hates the sin. That's why He could love me while I was in the very act of beating someone, shooting horse or pimping. He hated what I was doing; He hates evil so much He had to destroy it. That's why Jesus died on the cross. And He died for every type and form of sin, whether it's a horrible act of murder, or just putting a dent in our neighbor's car and driving away. This is why the person who commits heinous murders can be saved; it's also why the good church-goer can be saved. To God, there is simply no difference.

Once a year, I go back to Terre Haute, but not because I'm homesick. Brother Lindsey is still dashing around the halls of Terre Haute setting men on fire for Jesus. Years ago, the Lord told Brother Lindsey if he would stay in the prison ministry, He would send one man back each year to Terre Haute to minister during a revival. So each year, Brother Lindsey sponsors a revival for the men in the prison and some of the old brothers from the Brotherhood come for it. Brother Lindsey has been at this for 12 years to date; last year, 12 brothers met at Terre Haute for the revival. One for each year, just as the Lord promised. And it's not easy for the brothers to find the money to travel across the nation just to visit a place they hate! But somehow, each year, another brother we haven't seen for years shows up at Terre Haute for the revival. A new one each year.

It's hard to walk the same halls, see my old cell, see the empty faces on the prisoners, and to be reminded of the way I used to live. I also see men who were saved 10 years ago still serving time, some for the second sentence, because they won't get serious with the Lord. And the sound of those big steel doors closing *behind* me once again still sends a chill up my spine. The constant sound of clanging doors is responsible for the word "slammer" and it's a sound you quickly learn to hate. In spite of all that, I am reminded each year of how far the Lord has brought me.

I've seen 300 men at a time come forward to accept Jesus in prison chapels. I've seen men delivered of drugs. I've seen men go down on their knees in sin and get up a few minutes later looking like new men—like they literally had "face" surgery and God gave them new faces while they were down on their knees becoming His sons.

One of the most beautiful sights I've seen involved one big black brother who was a hardened killer and looked like one. He had eyes that were as cold as steel and his biceps looked like boulders. I preached in his prison and when I finished, he came running to the front with tears streaming down his cheeks. He wrapped his arms around this skinny preacher and cried like a baby. And he just kept saying, "Brother, my mama's prayers have been answered!" He made up about four of me, but all I could do was hug him back and say, "Praise the Lord!" During the service, God had just melted him and given him a heart made of putty; and now he remembered his mama's prayers.

I could picture some sweet little old saint sitting in her rocker and praying in a loud voice for her big wayward son. And I could hear her telling him, just like my mama told me, *"Son, I'm praying for you . . . God promised and I'm praying for you!"*